Better

A practical guide to
PAVING

FRANK GARDNER

MINI • WORKBOOK • SERIES

MURDOCH BOOKS®
Sydney • London • Vancouver • New York

CONTENTS

Slate edging with clay pavers (top), clay pavers (far left) and terracotta tiles (left)

Recycled house bricks laid in a herringbone pattern form a handsome feature of this compact courtyard. A circular bed at the centre accommodates an established crepe myrtle and simple foliage plants.

Planning your paving

Carefully laid paving can transform the exterior landscape of your home into a functional yet decorative setting for a range of occasions. Consider your needs before drawing up a plan.

WHEN TO PAVE

Paving enables you to move around outside the home and create specialist areas within your landscape design. Construct these low-maintenance, hard-surface areas before adding the softer embellishments of garden beds, plants and lawns.

Paths and driveways—the 'high traffic lanes'— are the most commonly paved areas around a home, but you can use paving to define outdoor living spaces such as courtyards, patios and pool surrounds and add colour and style by introducing patterns and texture.

Paving materials are especially useful where there are changes of level or drainage problems.

BENEFITS OF PAVING

Although there are many ways of providing hard-surface areas around your home, paving offers additional benefits to the home landscaper.

- Paving provides a hard-wearing, long-term surface with an attractive finish that weathers well.
- It can be used effectively in the formation of a path, driveway or entertainment area, directing movement or providing space in which to sit and relax.
- Correctly paved areas require little maintenance in any setting.
- Paving projects can be undertaken with success by the home landscaper.
- Paving materials come in a variety of styles and colours that blend or contrast with other surfaces such as lawn, garden beds and water.
- Paved areas can be used in either formal or informal settings.
- Pavers can be laid in a variety of patterns to cater for individual tastes.
- Paving materials are available to suit any situation or budget.

PLANNING

Paved areas are an extension of your living space, so plan to incorporate natural features such as trees, gardens and exposed rock surfaces to ensure your project is in harmony with its setting rather than imposed on it.

Begin by drawing a detailed plan of your house and land. Mark the key points such as entry doors, the garage, gates and specific parts of your garden that require connection via a path. Note the places where you like to relax or entertain, or areas that are shady or constantly damp. Plan to connect the proposed hard-surface areas around your home in an interesting but practical way.

Next, consider the shape and size of your proposed paving and the impact such areas will have on the appearance of your home.

DRIVEWAYS

A driveway is a focal point; in fact, it is often the first thing a visitor notices. Constructing a driveway to blend with the architectural style of the house and its garden setting is important. A straight driveway creates a formal approach to a home whereas a curved or sweeping driveway appears more inviting. A circular driveway, which becomes a feature when a garden, statuary or a pond is added, is an option on a wide-fronted block.

PATHS

Paved paths direct traffic and reduce the amount of dirt and mud carried in from outdoors. As well as leading visitors to the main entrance of the house, they provide protection for plants and lawn.

Straight paths give a formal and direct approach and usually lead to entrances, exits or work areas (such as a tool shed or clothes drying area). Meandering paths often blend with the garden and are designed to take the traveller on a leisurely stroll to a seat, courtyard or swimming pool.

ENTRIES

The entry to a home may incorporate a porch, a foyer, a verandah, steps or a ramp, all of which can be created with your choice of paving materials. Beautiful, tessellated tiled patterns have been a feature of verandahs and porches for many years. More recent styles have turned to the use of natural stone, slate, terracotta, ceramic and brick for an elegant yet hardwearing finish for entry areas and steps.

RELAXATION AREAS

Areas for home relaxation include patios, terraces, courtyards, barbecue surrounds and swimming pools. As these form a transition between the house and the garden, it is vital that the material and style work in harmony with the home.

WATER FEATURES

Pools and ponds are often set slightly apart from the home, swimming pools being separated from the main body of the yard by safety fencing. Garden ponds are usually situated in a shady corner designed as a restful nook. Paving is an ideal treatment for such areas, which are usually damp. Near swimming pools, it provides a safe non-slip surface and an attractive edge and coping material. Take special care as the chosen material must be tolerant of either salt or chlorine and other pool chemicals.

SHADY AREAS

Paving is ideal on damp or shaded ground where grass will not grow. Brighten areas overshadowed by large trees or buildings by installing a garden seat, fountain or statue on a firm surface of patterned pavers.

MAINTAINING YOUR PAVING

DISGUISING TREE ROOT DAMAGE

Uplifting or cracking by tree roots usually occurs over many years.

- If the tree cannot be moved or pruned, introduce a curve or circle to redirect the paving around the troubled area.
- If the damage affects only part of a long length of paving, create a slight, unobtrusive undulation to disguise it and maintain the existing direction. Re-lay the pavers in the damaged section and for several metres on both sides.

CORRECTING SINKAGE

Uneven sections appear in paving due to subsidence in the base material. Lift the surface layer of pavers, bricks or stone and correct minor sinkages by adding extra bedding sand. If the problem is significant, loosen the surface of the base material, rake in dry cement, recompact the base and replace the pavers.

CLEANING BRICK PAVING

Unsightly blemishes on paving can be removed with basic care.

- Efflorescence appears as a white, powdery discolouration on the surface of new bricks or pavers. It is the result of soluble salts being drawn to the surface by moisture. Remove efflorescence by dry brushing with a stiff-bristled brush or broom. Washing with a hose does not solve the problem as the offending crystals are simply dissolved back into the brickwork.
- Contain growths such as moulds, lichens and mosses by ensuring unnecessary moisture does not accumulate under paved surfaces. Expose affected areas to increased sunlight—thereby allowing them to dry out—by removing or pruning back overhanging plants or trees. Use a spade or stiff-bristled brush to scrub away the bulk of the material, then treat the area with a bleach or fungicidal solution.
- Wear protective clothing when using an acid-based wash for removing stains. A mixture of 10:1 water and hydrochloric acid is appropriate, but the acid can cause discolouration and damage some timbers and metals. As a last resort, lift, turn over and re-lay the pavers.

CLEANING STONE AND TILES

Earthenware tiles are difficult to stain and exposure to the elements usually keeps them clean. Around barbecues or where grease or oil spills are likely to occur, sealing is the most feasible option. Maintain slate and sandstone by sweeping regularly and washing with clean water, or mix 5 litres of water with 250 millilitres of chlorine bleach for use as a scrub.

Freshly laid clay pavers introduce the warmth of terracotta to this Mediterranean-style garden and brighten what could otherwise be a rather dim corner. Earthy, hard-wearing materials are ideal in shady locations such as this.

Basic materials

Modern pavers are available in clay, concrete, slate, marble, granite, sandstone and other manufactured finishes. Paving is also possible with standard house bricks or natural flagstones.

CHOOSING MATERIALS

Once you have decided where to pave, select the most suitable material for the job.

Some of the most common paving materials are:

- clay pavers
- house bricks
- concrete pavers
- slate or marble
- cut or split stone (such as sandstone)
- natural flagstones
- ceramic, terracotta or concrete tiles
- imitation sandstone, limestone, slate and granite
- granite setts

Consider the architectural style of your home, the degree of formality in your setting, your budget and the availability of materials. Non-slip surfaces are essential for paving exposed to the elements or in areas prone to dampness or moss growth.

CLAY PAVERS

The greater strength and hardness of clay pavers give them an advantage over house bricks and make them ideal for heavy traffic areas such as driveways. They are also better suited to use in corrosive situations such as around salt-water swimming pools. Consistently rectangular clay pavers can be tessellated to create a choice of patterns and, because they are flat on both sides, chipped corners can be hidden on the downward face.

Clay pavers are available in a variety of sizes, 230 x 115 x 50 mm being the most useful. As this width is exactly half the length, it is possible to create interlocking designs (such as basketweave) as well as standard paving patterns. Both clay pavers and house bricks come in warm, earthy colours, and clay, being a natural material, provides a richness that does not fade over time. In exposed situations, dark clay absorbs heat, becoming very hot, particularly in the summer. Light colours stay cooler and can make an area appear larger, but in damp, shaded areas or under shedding foliage, staining and moss growth become more apparent.

HOUSE BRICKS

House bricks (both new and old) are an alternative to commercial pavers. The rustic appeal of house bricks adds an 'old world' charm to any setting, particularly if you are able to purchase original sandstocks. They are best suited to courtyards, paths and patios and should not be used around swimming pools.

When combining materials, identify a common theme: here, it is the russet tones of the clay and slate.

Before using house bricks in driveways, discuss their suitability with the supplier.

House bricks usually measure 230 x 110 x 76 mm, so in an interlocking pattern such as basketweave the joints are slightly wider than usual as the length-to-width ratio is not exactly 2:1. Slight variations in dimension make positioning more difficult.

With their 76 mm depth, standard bricks require deeper excavation than is necessary when laying clay pavers. Dry pressed house bricks (or solids) have a frog in one side to assist in the bonding of the mortar bed, so each is left with only one possible exposed surface. Extruded house bricks (or wire cuts) are manufactured with holes running through their centres and must be laid on one edge, making them relatively fragile in use.

CONCRETE PAVERS

Standard pavers made from concrete—some available with spacing lugs on the sides— help make laying simple.

Modern, fade-resistant concrete pavers are often made to resemble natural products (such as sawn sandstone, slate, split granite and even terrazzo, with honed and polished surfaces). Many are manufactured as 20 mm thick tiles as well as 50 mm thick pavers.

The cobblestone has a time-worn appearance, particularly when the edges are rumbled. With its dimensions of approximately 230 x 190 x 50 mm, the cobblestone is unsuitable for some patterns (such as basketweave). Instead, choose from the range of geometric-shaped pavers, which are easier to lay in interlocking patterns.

Suitable for any paving pattern, the standard concrete paver (230 x 115 mm) is appropriate because of its 2:1 length to width ratio. For additional strength in driveways, irregular, interlocking pavers are produced in a variety of sizes and patterns. Concrete products vary in thickness. The thinner 40 mm pavers are ideal for pedestrian-only areas such as courtyards, terraces and swimming pool surrounds. For domestic driveways, a 50 mm thickness copes with normal traffic.

For heavier traffic in industrial and commercial situations, pavers of 60 mm thickness are recommended.

A new concrete product known as UrbanStone is manufactured from a mix of limestone, cement and aggregate wet-cast into moulds which vibrate mechanically to produce an extremely hard-wearing finish. The product has the texture and colour of natural stone but the strength of concrete. At 400 x 400 x 40 mm, the standard UrbanStone paver is much larger than a traditional paving block but does not suffer from loss of strength.

STONE

Any flat-surfaced rock is suitable for use as flagging.

- Igneous rocks (such as granite and basalt) are formed from molten magna or lave. Many of the early nineteenth-century cobbled streets were made from very hard basalt known as bluestone. Granite is a popular paving material, particularly as road inserts and in large public areas. The surface of granite is extremely hardwearing and durable but this stone is expensive.
- Sedimentary rocks (including limestone) are formed by the steady build-up of fossilised remains, seashells, sand or existing rock. Sandstone blocks (commonly 800 x 400 x 50 mm) are sold with one or both main surfaces sawn. Split sandstone is irregular in shape and is suited to a more informal setting. Although heavy, sandstone is a soft material, easy for the home paver to cut and lay. New sandstone weathers quickly, as it is porous, and it soon begins to appear aged. Sandstone's natural non-slip surface provides an excellent built-in safety element. It is a popular material for steps, courtyards, verandahs, paths and patios and can be laid safely around chlorinated swimming pools.
- Metamorphic rocks are formed by heat or pressure resulting from movement of the earth's crust. The best-known examples are marble and slate. Marble chips are used in terrazzo floors and paving.

SLATE

Slate is created by the compression of clays, shales and volcanic ash and can be split along planes of cleavage to thicknesses of as little as 5 mm. As a metamorphic rock with low porosity, it is generally difficult to stain. The exception occurs when slate is laid around a barbecue, where it is exposed to oil and grease spills.

Most commercial slates originate in Africa, China, Britain, Belgium, Spain, India or Italy. In Australia, importers deal largely in the best-quality slate from Africa, which makes it expensive to buy. It comes in dark mottled tones of black, gold and red and, as darker colours absorb heat, this slate is most suited to interior or shaded areas. For open exterior paving, lighter coloured slate (such as the Chinese or Indian varieties) is recommended. Chinese slate is available in tones ranging from brown to green and is suitable for use in outdoor situations (including in and around swimming pools). Some Chinese green slate is rich in iron pyrites or 'fool's gold'.

The Indian type of slate is usually a combination of mottled brown, pink, silver and red. The Indian variety is cheaper than African slate but often contains iron oxide, making it unsuitable for use around pools and in other wet situations in which rust staining occurs. Australian slate is more expensive.

Slate tiles can be purchased with cut, handsawn or chipped edges. Cut-edged tiles are uniform in size and give a formal finish to paving. Handsawn slate varies slightly in dimension but has neat edges on both sides. Chipped slate is guillotined, causing breaking or chipping on one side. This means laying is usually restricted to only one surface, with the chipped side facing down.

TILES

Tiles are available in a wide price bracket and range from plain terracotta to complicated tessellated patterns and colours. Exterior tiles can be used for driveways and paths, in courtyards, on patios, terraces and verandahs, and around swimming pools. Made from concrete or clay, they come in a variety of colours, sizes and finishes.

- Concrete tiles made from finely crushed aggregate are fired at extremely high temperatures and are usually quite thick (approximately 15–20 mm), with a variety of texture finishes to replicate natural products. They have low porosity and high impact-resistance and offer a range of tessellating options when laid. Colours usually vary between batches, so when purchasing try to ensure your order is filled from a single source.
- Clay (or ceramic) tiles have been popular for years in many situations, both inside and out. Those suited to exterior use include terracotta and quarry tiles.

Quarry tiles have a rough surface, making them non-slip in exposed weather situations. Tiles made from terracotta (which is Italian for 'baked earth') have a porosity higher than that of concrete tiles, meaning they are more absorbent, a problem particularly around barbecues. Generally, their rough surface and fade-resistant, rich, earthy colours make them a popular choice for exterior use. Their usual thickness is 15 mm but irregularities sometimes occur. To maintain the non-slip quality and avoid trapping discolouration, leave terracotta tiles unsealed outdoors.

COMBINATIONS

Many paved areas combine two or more of the previously mentioned materials. A combination such as limestone pavers with a terracotta header or stone with a brick border creates an unusual yet harmonious result in the garden.

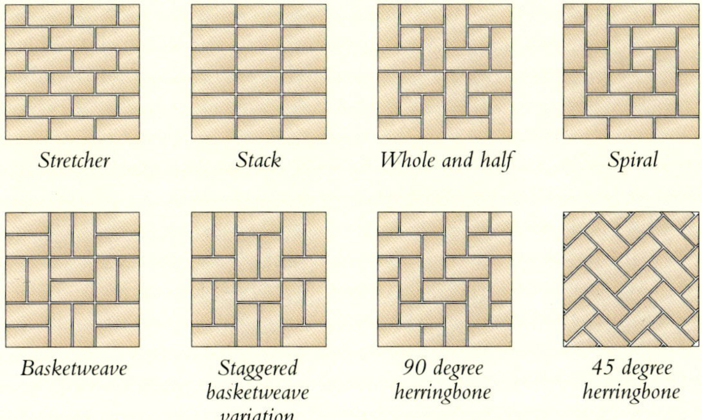

BRICK AND PAVER BONDS

BONDS

STACK

Stack is an easy bond to lay, but take care to maintain straight lines in both directions. This does not provide a strong bond and is unsuitable for driveways.

STRETCHER

Stretcher creates a strong bond which looks best as a meandering path between two header courses. It is also useful on large straight areas and curves and in unusual layouts.

HERRINGBONE

Herringbone is a strong, interlocking style that is particularly good for driveways and other high-use areas. The pattern fits easily into irregular shapes and tends to make paved areas look longer. If herringbone bond is laid at 45 degrees, you will need to cut a lot of bricks. Plan the layout carefully to ensure this time-consuming process is minimised.

BASKETWEAVE

Visually, this repeating pattern tends to 'close in' and reduce the apparent size of paved areas. It is most appropriate in square or rectangular situations as difficult cutting is required when adapting basketweave to curved edges.

SPIRAL

Spiral is an active pattern, creating movement from the centre.

PROVIDING AN EDGE

Any paved area requires an edge. Whether to lay this edge first or last is a personal decision often regulated by the material and pattern selected. The edge provides a perimeter to contain the paving, retain bedding sands and loose material, delineate

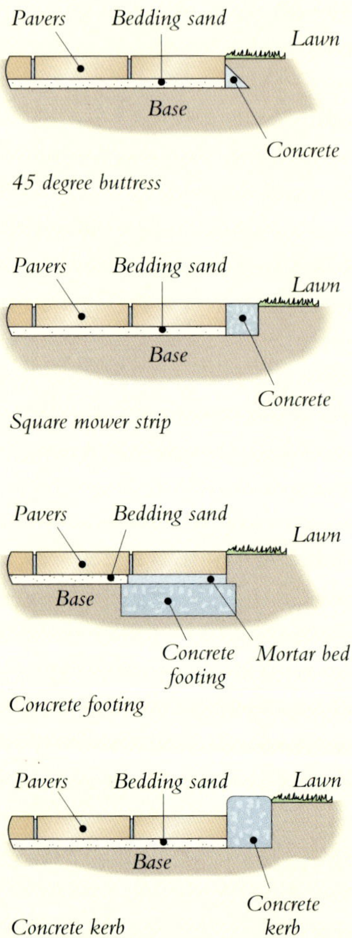

CONCRETE EDGINGS

other areas (such as garden beds) and even double as a mowing strip at the side of a lawn.

BRICK EDGING

The edge on brick paving, placed either square or lengthwise down the sides, is called the 'header course'. A header course, constructed with whole bricks which fully contain any smaller cut sections, strengthens the edge of the paving and adds a decorative finish when laid in a contrasting colour.

A square header course is laid at right angles to the paving; a longitudinal header course or 'soldier course' is laid parallel.

Raised brick edging acts as a kerb to retain garden beds or direct the flow of water.

CONCRETE EDGING

Driveway, path and courtyard surfaces often meet gardens or lawns and need strong edges to prevent movement, as any loss of soil from beneath the base eventually causes paving to sink.

- Create a buttress of 45 degrees. After laying your paving with brick or stone, cut away and remove any loose material down to the firm base. Place concrete against the edge bricks and, using a metal or wooden float, batter it at an angle of 45 degrees to form a buttress. The concrete should cover at least half the depth of the bricks. Once the light covering of topsoil is returned, surrounding plants or lawn can grow up to the edge of the paving.
- Install a square mower strip, formed in a similar way to a buttress.
- Include a concrete footing, enabling the concrete to be hidden from view while still acting as a retainer.

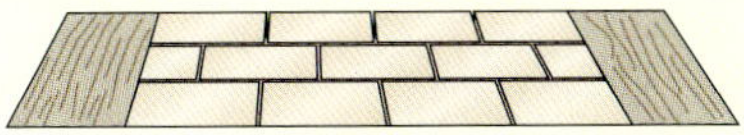

Timber border

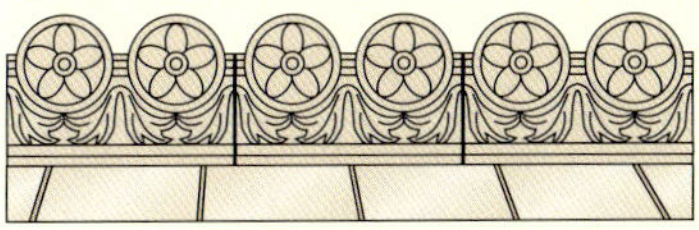

Ceramic tile border

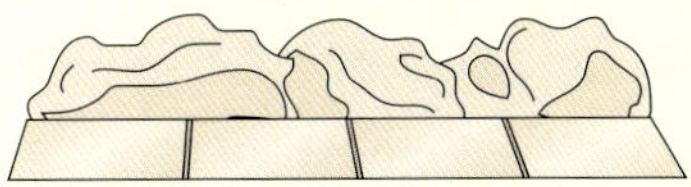

Sandstone border

Wire border

BORDERS

- Construct a concrete kerb to redirect water flow and/or retain an area higher than the paving.

TIMBER EDGING

Timber edging is useful for retaining loose paving materials such as bark and pebbles. Lay durable hardwood or preservative-treated pine with an H4 rating lengthwise along the path and fix it into position with wooden pegs and galvanised nails. Old railway sleepers can be laid to form retaining walls or seating. Drive the pointed ends of treated pine logs into the ground to form a vertical barrier.

TERRACOTTA TILE EDGING

The decorative terracotta edging tiles, which stand vertically and form interesting patterned edges, are enjoying a resurgence.

Rectangular border tiles are often used like a header course. A border of a different colour or with an inlaid frieze provides visual impact when used in moderation.

STONE AND ROCK EDGING

Rock and stone are excellent as hard edging and work equally well with paths of loose material, stepping stones and bricks. Stone or rock is effective along free-flowing and curved paths.

ALTERNATIVE EDGINGS

Historical influence or the unavailability of traditional materials in some areas prompts innovative approaches to edging. Glass, in the form of bottles (particularly large dark-coloured beer or wine bottles), is sometimes used as edging and in retaining walls. To construct a glass edge, stand the bottles vertically upside down and push them firmly into the soil, supported by a 45 degree concrete buttress. Be wary of using glass in areas accessible to children or where the bottles may be broken accidentally.

Victorian and Edwardian garden beds were edged with loops of wire. Today, these looped and woven wire borders are available in rolls of galvanised or PVC- or powder-coated wire in heritage colours.

Slabs of slate laid randomly in the popular 'crazy paving' style coordinate beautifully with traditional clay pavers around this freeform swimming pool. Thorough preparation is vital when attempting an advanced design.

Paving techniques

Whatever you decide to pave, the basic steps remain the same. In any project, the keys to success are careful planning and solid preparation of the site; paving is only ever as solid as its base.

CALCULATING AREA

Most paving materials are sold by the square metre (m^2).

SQUARE OR RECTANGULAR AREAS

Multiply the length by the width. For example, the surface area of a courtyard that measures 12 m long by 5 m wide equals:

$12 \times 5 = 60\ m^2$

To determine the number of bricks required, multiply the surface area (m^2) by forty (forty being the number of standard bricks to the square metre), thus:

$60 \times 40 = 2400$ bricks

CIRCULAR AREAS

Use the formula πr^2, where π equals 3.14 and r is the radius. For example, calculate the surface area of a paved circular feature with a radius of 4 m as follows:

$\pi \times r^2 = 3.14 \times 4^2 = 3.14 \times 16 = 50.24\ m^2$

TRIANGULAR AREAS

When working with a triangle, multiply half the base length by the height. For a triangular area 4 m wide at the base and 6 m high, the calculation is:

$(\frac{1}{2} \times 4) \times 6 = 2 \times 6 = 12\ m^2$

BASIC TOOLS

- Stringline
- Measuring tape
- Spirit level
- Straight edge
- Shovel
- Spade
- Rake
- Hammer
- Rubber mallet
- Hand saw
- Screed rails and board
- Steel float
- Permanent black marking pen
- Lump hammer
- Bolster
- Wheelbarrow
- Broom
- Hose and nozzle

COMBINATION AREAS

For areas involving a combination of shapes, calculate each component individually, then simply add the totals together. For example, if the area of a terrace comprises a square and a triangle, sketch the area and divide it with a dotted line (see Combination areas, page 18).

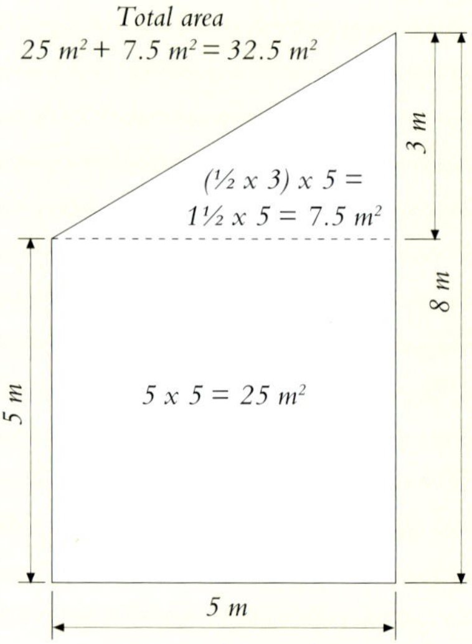

COMBINATION AREAS

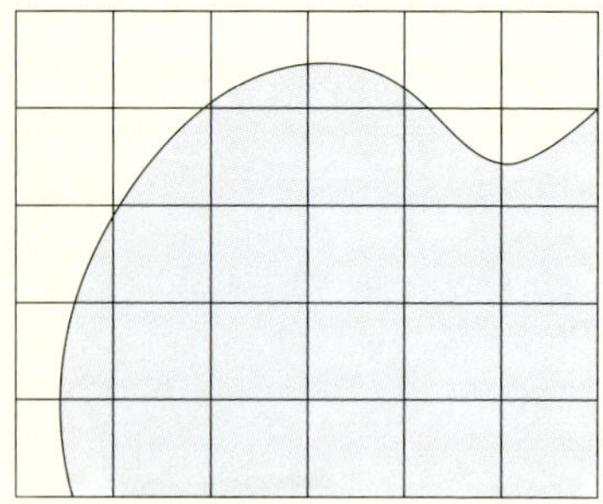

IRREGULAR AREAS

Calculate the square area:
length x width = 5 x 5 = 25 m^2
then calculate the triangular area:
½ base x height = (½ x 3) x 5 =1.5 x 5 = 7.5 m^2
As the final step, add the two area subtotals together:
25 m^2 + 7.5 m^2 = 32.5 m^2

IRREGULAR AREAS

Estimate irregularly sized areas by sketching the outline of your proposed paving carefully onto squared paper, with each square representing 1 m^2 as shown in the diagram above right.
Add up the whole square metres:
m^2 = 17
Even-out the part-square metres by combining them:
m^2 = 5

Always round partial metres up to a full-metre to allow for wastage from cut or broken pavers. Thus:
17 + 5 = 22 m^2

ORDERING MATERIALS

Shop around for the best value on price or look for discounted products.

- Brick supply companies sell house bricks and clay and concrete pavers. Original sandstocks and footpath paving bricks are sometimes available second-hand from demolition yards. These are sold by the square metre or by the thousand. When converting from one to the other, remember that there are 40 standard house bricks per square metre. Thus, 1000 bricks/40 = 25 m^2
- Tiles and slate are sold by the square metre. Select only tiles suitable for exterior use if your paving will be exposed to the weather.
- Sandstone can be purchased new, secondhand or in an artificial form.

Ensure the stone chosen for your project is at least 50 mm thick.

• Various other materials (such as limestone pavers) are available from landscape and paving supply centres.

• Bedding material, usually in the form of sand, can be ordered by the tonne or by the cubic metre. A rule-of-thumb correlation is 1.5 tonnes to 1 m^3 of bedding sand. The material should be either coarse and natural (such as washed river sand) or a manufactured by-product of quarry crushing processes (packing sand).

To calculate your order, multiply the square metre surface area by the depth of the bedding. For example, when laying a 25 mm bed over an area of 20 m^2, calculate:

20 m^2 x a depth of 0.025 m = 0.5 m^3

then apply the rule-of-thumb correlation:

0.5 m^3 x 1.5 = 0.75 tonnes

Double-check your calculations, then order a little extra to allow for slight variations in the depth of your bed.

• The ultimate base material for paving is concrete. Ready-mixed concrete is sold by the cubic metre (m^3). To calculate your needs, multiply the surface area by the depth proposed (usually 100 mm). For example, a rectangular area 12 x 5 m requires:

12 x 5 x 0.1 = 6 m^3

An alternative to concrete is a base of crushed rock, sold by the tonne through landscape supply centres or directly from quarries. To order, calculate the cubic metres required (as for concrete), then multiply this by 1.5 to give an approximate tonnage (as for bedding sand). Thus:

12 m x 5 m x 0.1 m = 6 m^3, and

6 m^3 x 1.5 = 9 tonnes

This type of base is considerably cheaper than concrete (about 20 per cent of the cost) but it does have to be compacted thoroughly to reduce the risk of future sinkage.

• You may need small amounts of other materials, including washed beach sand and cement, for grouting, and concrete for edging.

MIXING CONCRETE

Order concrete ready-mixed or mix it on site by hand. The most common blend comprises four parts coarse aggregate (gravel), two parts fine aggregate (preferably river sand), one part cement, and sufficient water to produce a workable consistency. Coarse aggregate (in sizes of up to 20 mm) gives concrete its strength but for convenience use the 10 mm size, as this is easier to work.

If you require a large volume or do not want to mix your own, contact a local supplier ahead of time. Ready-mixed concrete is delivered in increments of 0.2 m^3. For example, standard quantities include 1.2 m^3, then 1.4 m^3, 1.6 m^3 and so on.

The composition of ready-mixed concrete is controlled by Standards Australia. For paths, driveways and slabs not supporting structures, a strength of twenty megapascals is required. To order concrete for a paving base, request a mix of

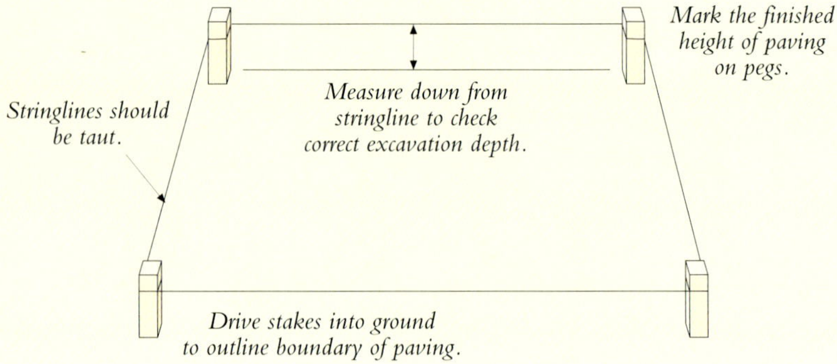

SETTING STRINGLINES

N20/10 ('N' denoting normal, '20' denoting twenty megapascals of strength and '10' denoting aggregate 10 mm in diameter).

CALCULATING QUANTITY

Concrete quantities are calculated by the cubic metre (m^3).

Usually, 1 m^3 quantity of concrete comprises 1 m^3 of coarse aggregate, 0.5 m^3 of fine aggregate, eight bags of cement and water as required.

The area covered is determined by the thickness of the slab. For example, when laid to a depth of 100 mm, 1 m^3 covers 10 m^2.

To calculate concrete by volume, multiply the length by the width by the depth of the given area. For a 10 x 1.5 m slab 0.1 m deep, you require 1.5 m^3.

Typically, this quantity is made up of:

- 1.5 m^3 of coarse aggregate
- 0.75 m^3 of fine aggregate
- twelve bags of cement
- water as required

MARKING OUT

Mark out the area, placing a peg in each corner or at each change of angle. On the pegs, indicate the desired finished height of the paving material.

Consider the slope of the land to ensure the finished paving drains adequately in the desired direction. Sloping or ramped sites pose few problems (ramped areas having natural run-off) but if your site is level you must create crossfall on the area to displace water quickly while controlling its flow. Usually a fall of 20 mm per metre is sufficient.

COPING WITH A SLOPE

If your site is not level and is too steep for ramping, introduce steps.

When deciding whether a ramp or series of steps is needed, calculate the rate of incline. Measure the length of the area, then run a stringline from one end to the other, fixing it at ground level at the high point.

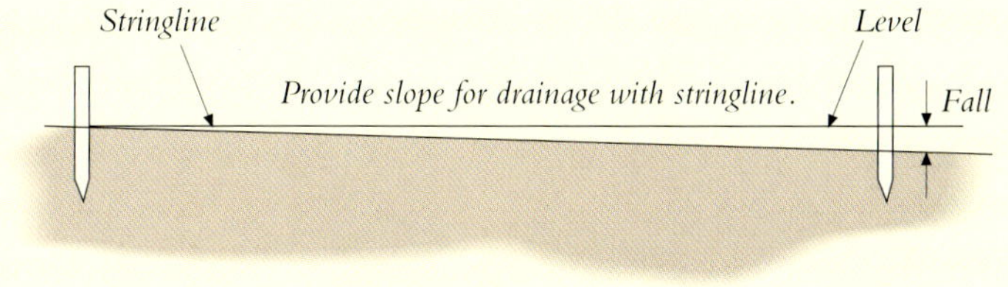

PROVIDING FALL

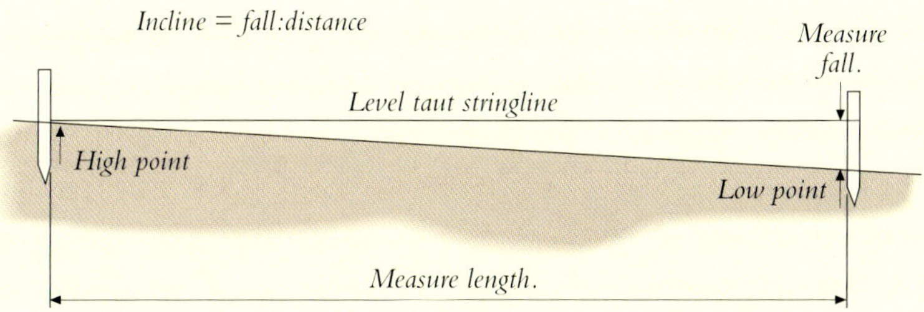

CALCULATING INCLINE

Stretch the stringline taut and horizontal. At the low point, measure the distance from the stringline to the ground to determine the amount of fall. Compare that to the distance, to obtain the rate of incline. As a guide, ramps may be used when the rate does not exceed 1:10 (that is, a 1 m fall over a 10 m length of path). If the slope is greater than 1:10, it is usually more appropriate to build steps.

EXCAVATION AND BASE PREPARATION

Having set the finished-height stringlines, excavate the area to the appropriate depth. Stretch a taut stringline from one side to the other at the desired paving edge height. Measure from the stringline to the surface, adjusting the soil as required.

Once the excavation is complete, check that the base is solid. If you locate soft spots, particularly in clay-based soils (due to poor drainage or broken pipes), dig them out. Redirect drainage or repair broken pipes before paving begins. Alternatively, rake cement through the existing base material, compact it firmly, hose the surface lightly and allow it to set.

Always work on a solid base to reduce the threat of future sinkage.

Paving that carries only pedestrian traffic rarely requires a concrete or compacted base; unless the soil is clay-based and has drainage problems, simply lay the paving material straight onto a 25–50 mm depth of screeded bedding sand.

SCREEDING

Screeding is the technique of levelling bedding sand to remove the dips and bumps that would otherwise give the paving an uneven surface.

RAISED RAIL METHOD

Place timber edges or rails at the finished stringline height and peg or nail them into position. Select a straight piece of timber (usually 100 x 50 mm in dimension) long enough to cover the width of the area to be screeded. Cut a notch from each end, 8–10 mm shallower than your chosen paver. (This allows for compaction once the paving is in use.) Draw the screed board along the rails. Ensure the bedding is packed firmly. Use a metal float to push back or remove the build up of sand that occurs behind the board.

BEDDED RAIL METHOD

This is probably the easier method, as less preparation and fewer materials are required.

Use screed rails made from aluminium or PVC conduit, water pipe, or timber, bedded into the sand. (For narrow areas, only one rail is necessary.) Ensure the rails are below the finished string height by the same thickness as that of your bricks, less 8–10 mm. (Check this by placing one of your selected bricks on a screed rail and measuring its height against the stringline. The top should protrude 8–10 mm.) Drag a straight piece of timber or large spirit level steadily along the rails, screeding off and packing the sand to create a firm, level laying surface. Remove the rails and use a float to fill the grooves with sand.

CURVED PAVING

Curves soften the landscape, invite leisurely, relaxed movement and make areas appear longer, particularly when you walk or glance down a meandering path, around a swimming pool or along a driveway.

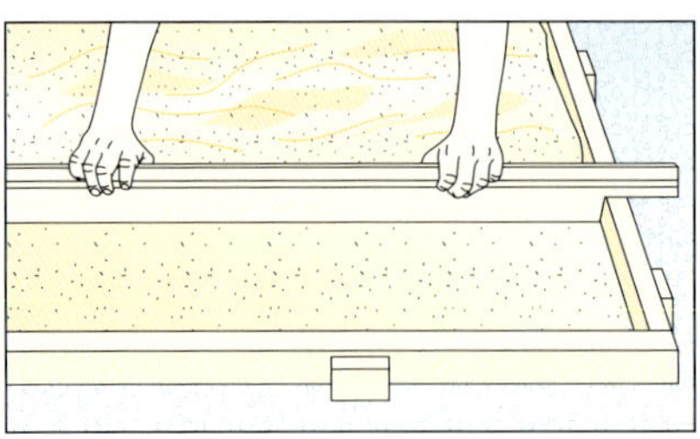

Draw a notched screed board along two raised rails. Ensure the bedding sand is packed firmly.

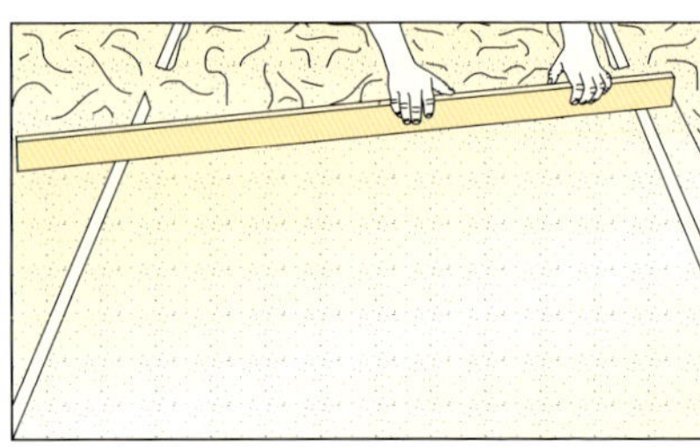

Bed the screed rails into the sand. Draw a straight edge or spirit level along the rails, levelling the surface.

Curves are also useful for their capacity to work within an established garden landscape, accommodating obstacles such as rocky outcrops and large trees or shrubs you don't want to move.

If you choose to create a curved driveway, allow space for drivers to manoeuvre vehicles. Sharp curves are not compatible with areas demanding sweeping movement and parking or reversing bays.

Form rectangular or square pavers into a natural, free-flowing shape by including a header course—a border separate to the paving and laid, therefore, at any angle. If you want your paving to reflect a curve, choose stretcher bond as your pattern. This eliminates cutting as the pattern bends to follow the paving line. In other common patterns, the bulk of the paving is laid independently of the header, which follows a scribed curve.

FOLLOWING A CURVE

Position a length of hose or rope as a guide. Look at the curve from all angles, adjusting it until you are satisfied that any straight spots have been removed.

Lay the header bricks on one side, following the curve created by your line. Use this as a laying guide for the remainder of your paving, following the curved header with stretcher bond.

Lay the stretcher courses evenly, checking the lines and adjusting the joints to keep the curve smooth.

PAVING TO A CURVE

This method involves considerable cutting but allows you to choose from a wide variety of patterns and is suitable for areas of any size. With the exception of swimming pools, for which the header is laid first, large areas of paving are completed before the curved header is put into place.

Lay the paving to just past the boundary of your intended edging. Use a hose or length of rope to create a free-flowing curve across the surface. With a permanent marking pen, scribe this line onto the pavers.

Remove any surplus paving from outside the curve, then lift the marked pavers, numbering each paver individually to simplify the replacement process. Cut the pavers neatly where marked and reposition them in sequence, using the numbers as a guide.

Place your chosen header pavers around the curve, ensuring the back edge of each is aligned with the cut edge.

CIRCULAR PAVING

Paving circular areas can be more difficult and is usually more time-consuming than working with standard rectangular shapes.

Setting up requires careful planning, patterning is more complicated, and the need for careful brick-cutting cutting is increased. Perseverence is rewarded, as circular paving looks fabulous when completed, but before attempting a

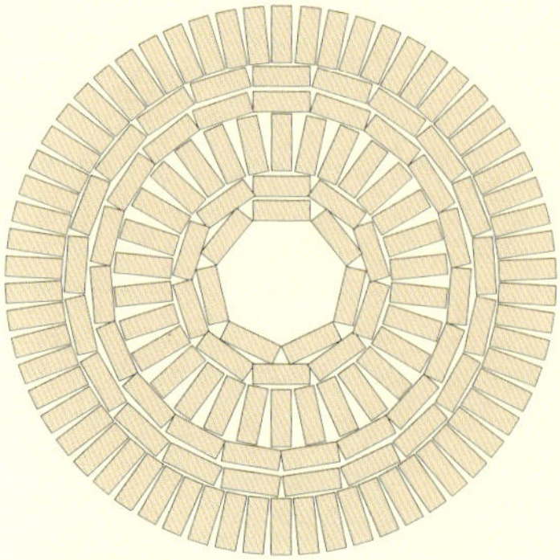

Double stretcher followed by a single header course

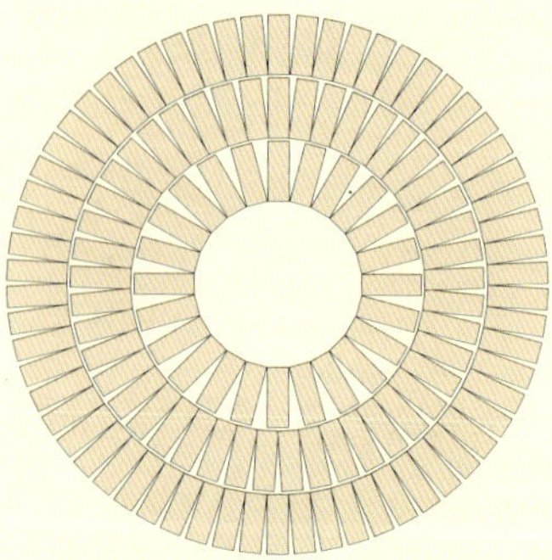

Radiating header courses

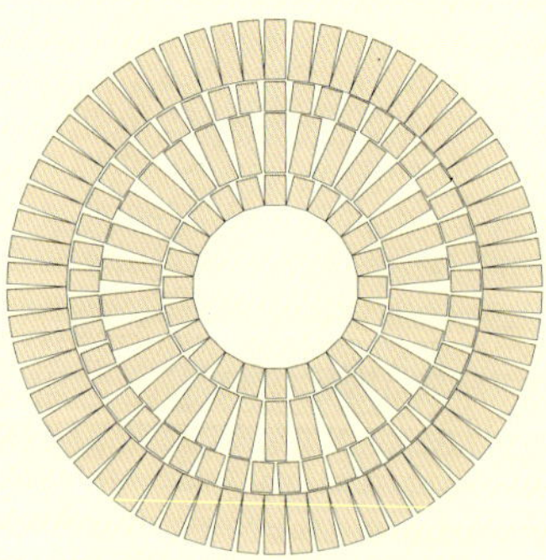

Half stretcher followed by single header course

CIRCULAR PATTERNS

circular design, make sure you obtain some practical experience with basic paving techniques.

Circular courtyards or features between two or more radiating paths form focal points in the landscape.

Sketch ideas onto paper and construct a sample to make sure your plan is feasible. Patterns that work effectively in circular areas include radiating headers, a single header plus a double stretcher, and crazy paving in stone.

LAYING THE PATTERN

The two basic methods for laying circular paving are outside-in and inside-out.

- To pave outside-in, place a peg at the centre of the site and attach a stringline to a nail at the top. With the string held taut, use a stick tied to the end to scribe a circle on the base. Beginning at the scribed line, work inwards. As the design tightens towards the centre, cut your bricks or pavers, if desired, or leave the area unpaved (and, perhaps, filled with plants) as a centrepiece.
- Inside-out paving is the more difficult method as it involves working in the confined space of the centre with your supply of materials outside the circle. Screed the area, then lay a plank across the sand as a makeshift walkway to provide access to your materials. Alternatively, avoid disturbing a screeded area by completing one full half of the circle before beginning the other section. Ensure the halves match up exactly.

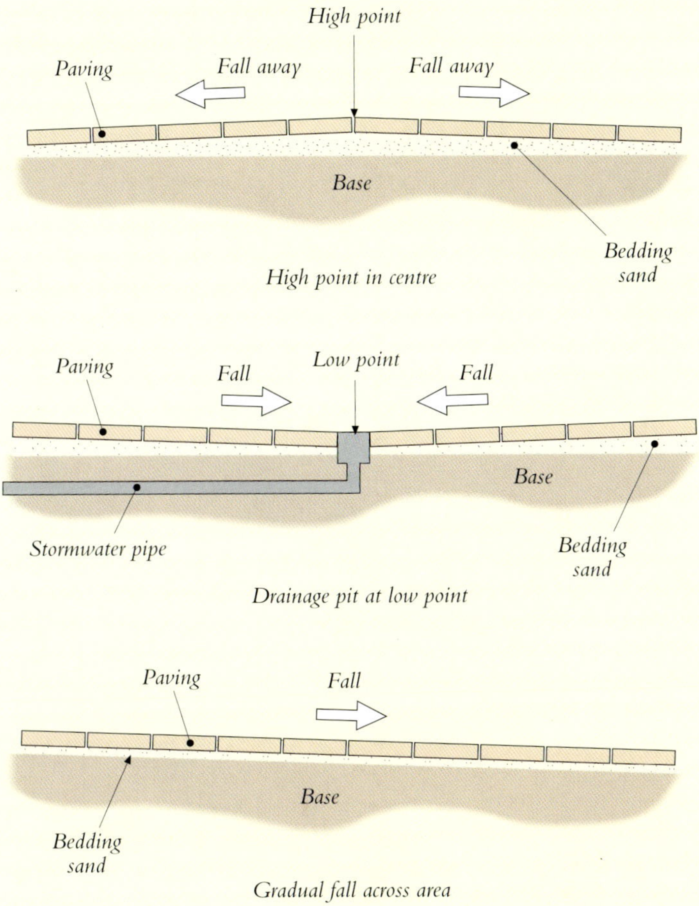

DRAINAGE

DRAINAGE FOR CIRCLES

Without correct fall, surface water will pool in the centre of your paving, making the area impractical for users and encouraging sinkage.

- On a level site, make the centre of the circle the high point, providing an even degree of fall away in all directions. Manipulate the fall by adding extra bedding material where required to create a gentle slope.
- On a sloping site, create a gradual fall across the width of the area.
- As an alternative on sloping ground, make the centre of the circle the low point and install a drain and subterranean pipework to remove excess water.

Pavers in light-traffic areas such as patios can be laid on a relatively inexpensive base of sand. Occasional sweeping with a stiff-bristled brush or broom is usually all that's required by way of maintenance.

Clay paving on sand

Laying pavers on a simple bed of sand is appropriate in areas that carry pedestrian traffic (such as paths, courtyards, barbecue areas, shady spots, patios and terraces).

PREPARATION

It is not necessary to place a base material beneath bedding sand provided the area drains freely and does not contain reactive, clay-based soil. A 45 degree buttress of concrete, suitable for most paving jobs, is one of the simplest edges to install.

1 Mark out the area, allowing for sufficient fall (preferably away from the house and towards grass, gardens, kerbs or drainage systems).

2 Set stringlines to the finished height (see page 20).

3 Excavate below the stringlines to at least 75 mm for clay pavers or 100 mm for house bricks.

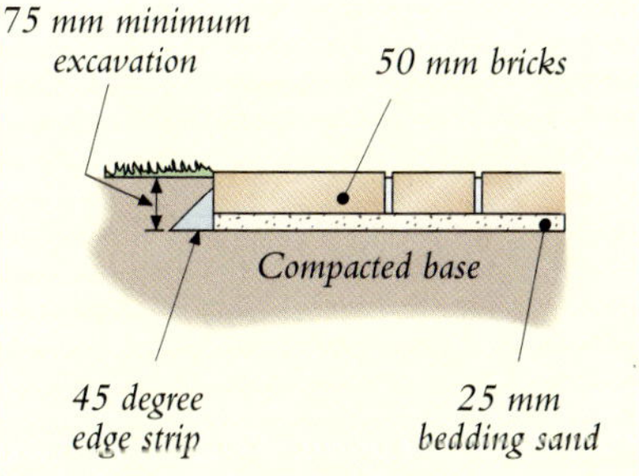

PAVING ON A SAND BASE

MATERIALS

- Clay pavers (or house bricks)
- Coarse-grained bedding sand
- Concrete mix for edging
- Fine-grained sand and/or soil for grout
- Cement

TOOLS

- Basic tool kit (see page 17)
- Brick saw or angle grinder for cutting bricks (optional)

4 Spread a 25 mm depth of bedding sand and rake it until it is roughly level. Screed using the method most suited to your work site (see Screeding, page 22).

LAYING

5 Laying pavers from an appropriate point saves a lot of cutting later. For example, if the proposed paving travels along two walls of your home and around a square corner, work outwards in both directions from the corner to avoid the cutting nightmare created by having a pattern meet there. Lay pavers against solid structures first, then proceed

out into an open space, again to prevent having to cut the final row.

6 Set up taut stringlines to guide your paving. Measure a small, loosely laid sample area to determine an accurate spacing.

7 If practical, lay a header course to provide a starting point (see Providing an edge, pages 13–15.)

8 Always lay pavers to set stringlines—do not simply butt them up to one another. Leave a small gap to accommodate variations in paver dimensions and keep the lines straight. Pavers need room for expansion and movement, so create a joint of 1–2 mm. Fit the pavers loosely to allow for minor adjustments and grouting.

CUTTING

9 Once the whole pavers are in place, you may be left with space to be filled to complete the pattern. Before cutting a paver, mark it clearly. Place the paver across the space so that it sits on the surrounding surface. Scribe a line at the correct angle, approximately 5 mm in from what you consider to be a tight fit.

10 Cut the paver using a bolster and lump hammer, a block splitter, an angle grinder with a masonry blade or a brick saw.

- If using a bolster and lump hammer, place the paver on a firm bed of sand and tap around the four sides until it cracks.
- Block splitters or guillotines work best with cobblestones or house bricks, the compression action of the splitter tending to shatter pavers of baked clay.
- It is difficult to keep angle grinder cuts straight. Support each paver within a framework. Cut part way through the paver, place a bolster in the cut and tap sharply with a lump hammer to create a clean break.
- Brick saws with diamond-tipped blades are ideal for cutting large numbers of pavers quickly and neatly. Hire a saw on a four-hourly or daily basis. To avoid excessive charges, have your material marked

8 Always lay pavers carefully to set stringlines—do not simply butt them up to one another.

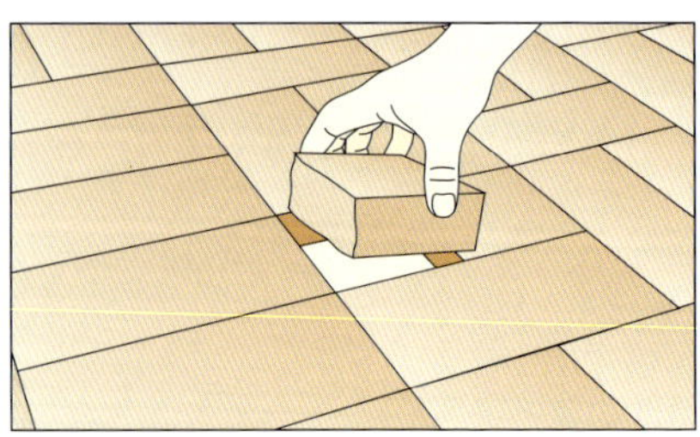

11 Insert each part-paver into the appropriate space with the cut edge facing the header course.

ready for cutting before collecting the machine.

- Use a scutch hammer to trim the cut surfaces of soft house bricks.

11 Insert each part-paver into its space with the cut edge facing the header course.

COMPACTING

12 Check that the line of pavers is straight and make your final adjustments. Compact the paving by hand or machine. Use a piece of timber or other straight edge as an anchor to hold the edge pavers in place to prevent them moving.

EDGING

13 With a spade or float, cut the bedding sand away from the edge pavers, exposing the solid base.

14 Mix up a quantity of concrete.

15 Shovel concrete along the exposed paver edge.

16 Use a float to batter the mixture to a 45 degree angle, ensuring it covers at least half the thickness of each paver. Allow the concrete to set completely.

> HINT
>
> If you choose to substitute standard house bricks for clay pavers in this project, remember to take into account the difference in depth when excavating and laying the base.

GROUTING

17 Use a fine-grained washed beach sand, sifted soil or a combination of six parts sharp sand to one part dry cement between the pavers. Ensure the paving is dry, then throw the grout mix over the surface.

18 Use a firm-bristled broom to push the grout into the joints. Sweep away the excess, reserving it for topping up the joints as required at a future date. (When cement powder is included, finish the process by hosing the surface with a very fine spray of water.)

12 Check that the line of pavers is straight and make your final adjustments. Compact the paving.

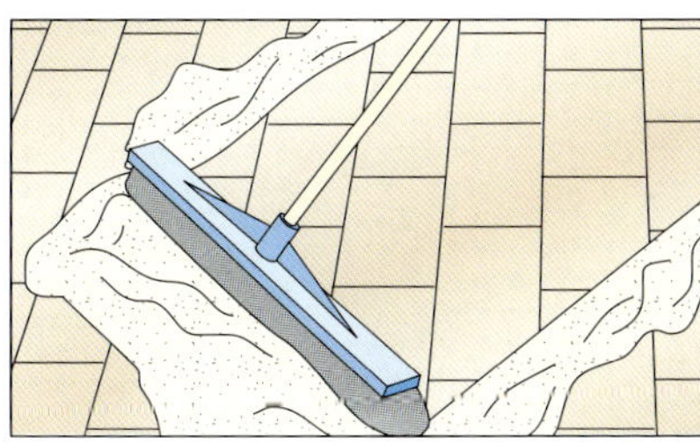

18 Use a broom to push the grout into the joints. Reserve the excess for topping up at a future date.

Clay paving on crushed rock

Heavy traffic areas such as driveways require the stability provided by a crushed rock base. This method is also suitable for land with drainage problems or reactive clay-based soils.

PREPARATION

In areas such as driveways, carports, swimming pools and moisture-laden spots with poor drainage, lay a solid base material beneath bedding sand. Crushed rock (known as roadbase) is about one-fifth the cost of concrete.

1 Mark out the area, allowing for sufficient fall (see pages 20–1).

2 Set stringlines and excavate.

3 Spread roadbase to a depth of approximately 100 mm. Rake or screed the surface. Measure the base height against the stringline and adjust the level of filling if necessary.

4 Hose the area lightly to moisten the surface and minimise dust.

TOOLS

- Basic tool kit (see page 17)
- Brick saw or angle grinder for cutting bricks (optional)

MATERIALS

- Clay pavers or house bricks
- Bedding sand
- Roadbase
- Concrete mix for edging
- Fine-grained sand for grout
- Cement

5 Compact the roadbase by machine.

6 Hose the area thoroughly and allow it to dry. When dry, the base should be almost rock hard.

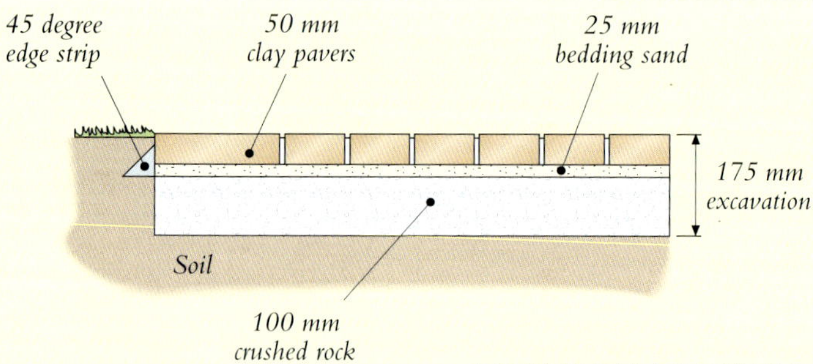

PAVING ON A ROCK BASE

Laying clay pavers or bricks on a base of crushed rock eliminates the threat of contact with reactive clay-based soils and minimises the possibility of sinkage on poorly drained land.

7 Spread bedding sand over the base to a depth of approximately 25 mm. Rake until roughly level, then screed using your preferred method.

PAVING

8 Follow standard procedures for laying, cutting, compacting, edging and grouting (see Clay paving on sand, pages 27–29).

HINT

Crushed rock is both dense and heavy, making it difficult to shovel and barrow into position. If your area is large, follow the lead of the professionals and hire a bobcat to move and spread your base.

A solid concrete slab provides the ultimate base for clay paving. Not only does concrete insulate pavers against the soil, it helps prevent upheaval by tree roots and sinkage due to waterlogging should a nearby drainage pipe begin to leak.

Clay paving on concrete

Pave on a base of concrete for extra stability around swimming pools, along driveways and in carports, parking bays and problem drainage areas. Plan to allow adequate curing time for the slab.

TOOLS

- Basic tool kit (see page 17)
- Jointing tool
- Wire twitcher or pliers
- Cement mixer (if mixing your own)
- Square-nosed shovel
- Gumboots
- Edger
- Wooden float

MATERIALS

- Clay pavers or house bricks
- Timber formwork
- Timber pegs
- Nails
- 75 mm expansion material (such as Jointex)
- F62 reinforced mesh, plus chairs
- Tie wire
- Concrete
- Fine-grained sand or grout

HINT

When ordering ready-mixed concrete, ensure adequate access is available for its delivery and that a clear wheelbarrow track is available from the driveway to the intended work site. Remove any obstacles which might hinder easy transportation of the load.

PREPARATION

1 Mark out the area, allowing for sufficient fall in the desired direction (preferably away from buildings).

2 Set stringlines at the desired finished height. Excavate the area to a minimum depth of 175 mm when laying conventional clay pavers or 200 mm if you elect to work with standard house bricks.

3 Build the formwork (see Erecting formwork, page 34). For straight edges, use 100 x 50 mm or 75 x 50 mm timber. When following a curved design, use 100 x 10 mm oregon offcuts which, although quite strong, are remarkably flexible.

4 If any part of the excavated area within the formwork is uneven and therefore requires filling, use clean sand screeded carefully to an appropriate level.

ERECTING FORMWORK

If your slab will rise above ground level, it will be necessary to construct formwork to contain the concrete. Formwork is a temporary structure, usually of timber or plywood, that holds wet concrete to the required shape until it has hardened.

Use long pieces of timber (such as oregon offcuts, which are flexible around curves), held in place with stakes on the outer sides. Use a spirit level to check that the formwork is level. Brace the formwork well to withstand the pressure of the heavy concrete.

5 If desired, place plastic sheeting into the excavation to prevent moisture rising through the concrete. This precaution is recommended for sheltered slabs but is not necessary in exposed situations.

6 Place F62 reinforcing mesh into position inside the formwork. Overlap the steel mesh by at least one-and-a-half to two squares and set it 50 mm in from the formwork edging. Join the mesh securely with tie wire, using either a pair of pliers or a wire twitcher.

7 If laying a slab against brickwork or another solid structure, place an expansion material (such as Jointex) against the wall at the finished concrete height. Fix this firmly in place by nailing through it and into a brick joint.

LAYING A SLAB

8 Barrow concrete into position. Spread and compact it using a square-nosed shovel.

9 Fill the excavation to the mid-way point. Lift the steel mesh to the surface of the still-wet slab and continue adding concrete until it reaches the desired level. As an alternative, support the steel mesh on reinforcement chairs.

10 Using a shovel or sturdy bricklayer's trowel, pack the wet

6 Place reinforcing mesh into position. Overlap the steel by at least one-and-a-half to two squares.

11 Move a straight edge back and forth to level the concrete against the top of the formwork.

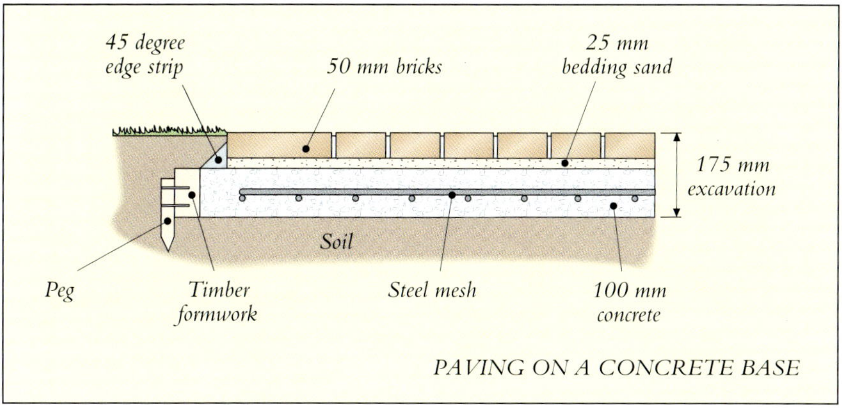

concrete tightly against the edges and into the corners of the formwork. Remove all air pockets.

11 Screed the concrete using a timber or aluminium straight edge. Move the straight edge slowly back and forth in a sawing motion to level the concrete against the top of the formwork, as though following the raised rail method (see Screeding, page 22). Do not edge the base slab.

12 Cut tool joints to prevent uncontrolled cracking over time. Run grooves at regular intervals across the surface, using a straight edge as a guide.

13 The surface of the concrete need not be particularly smooth. Finish the slab with a wooden float.

14 Allow the concrete to set and keep it wet for two or three days before removing the formwork.

PAVING

15 Lay clay pavers onto screeded bedding sand or use flexible adhesive to attach them directly to the slab (see pages 38–41).

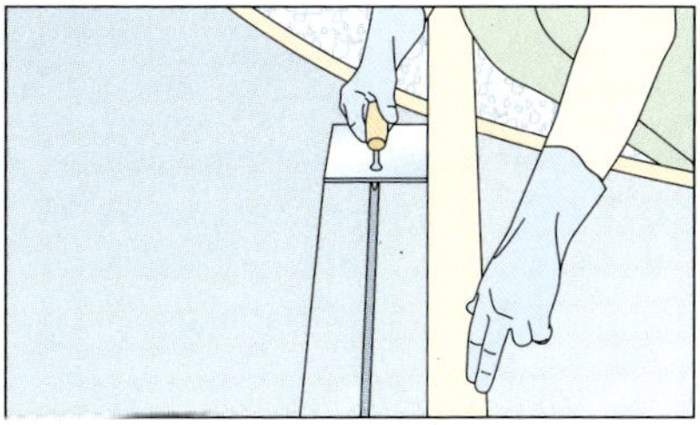

12 Cut tool joints at regular intervals across the surface of the concrete, using a straight edge as a guide.

13 The surface of the concrete need not be particularly smooth. Finish the slab with a wooden float.

PLANNING A DRIVEWAY

Make driveways wide and welcoming. Usually 3–3.5 m is wide enough to accommodate a car and give ample room for people to stand and walk on both sides of the vehicle.

Circular drives have a stately appearance and usually curve at the front entrance to the house. They require a broad frontage. A straight driveway has a direct, formal appearance while a sweeping drive creates a more informal atmosphere and usually has access at one side to provide extra parking space.

CHOOSING A BASE

Choose a base material with the compressive strength needed to support the weight of vehicles turning and stopping. If the base remains solid and free of weaknesses, the surface layer of paving—when laid correctly—will do likewise.

REGULATIONS

Before laying a driveway, request a copy of your local government authority's relevant regulations. Some councils demand that steel reinforcement be laid in the base which runs from the kerb to the property boundary. Some specify that the slab must be at least 100 mm thick, with F62 mesh embedded in the base. This depth increases to 150 mm if mesh is not used. Inspection may be required before the concrete is poured. Some councils even insist that the public land from the kerb to the boundary have a set degree of fall to the street with a flat area for the footpath. Check carefully to avoid having to re-lay a driveway that fails to meet official specifications.

PATTERNS

The strongest bonds are provided by interlocking patterns such as 45 degree and 90 degree herringbone. Header courses form a border to contain the natural lateral spread of paved surfaces under pressure.

COPING WITH SLOPE

Next, consider the lie of your land. Constructing a level driveway is simple compared to working on a steep site. On sloping land, providing traction (particularly in wet weather) is essential. Select a rough-textured paver to maximise tyre grip. Avoid laying tiles or stamped concrete with sealed surfaces, as these become slippery when wet and are extremely dangerous.

When steep driveway access is through a dip or over a sudden

Clay pavers laid in tough, interlocking patterns such as the herringbone variations provide an ideal surface for carports and driveways.

rise, the exhaust system or tow bar of some vehicles may drag or scrape on the paving surface. Prevent this by adjusting the curve during excavation. Dig out the driveway, then drive your car in and out to check for clearance problems before construction begins.

Negotiation with an adviser from your local council may be necessary if you want to alter the degree of fall to the kerb.

DRAINAGE

Steep driveways that drain towards a house or building need special consideration. To prevent surface water gushing into a garage at the base of the drive, install an open or grated drain.

For slightly sloping sites, incorporate a dish drain at the low point of the paving. Finish the driveway with a small (25 mm) step up into the garage or building to prevent entry of water.

Terracotta tile paving

Lay paving tiles on a reinforced concrete base. Pour the slab well before your paving project is scheduled to begin, as newly poured concrete requires adequate curing time.

TOOLS

- Basic tool kit (see page 17)
- 10 mm notched trowel
- Bolt cutters or angle grinder
- Rubber squeegee
- Rubber gloves
- Sponges
- Pliers or wire twitcher
- Buckets
- Chalkline
- Tile pincers
- Builder's square
- Wooden float
- Tile cutter, brick saw or angle grinder with diamond blade

MATERIALS

- 100 x 50 mm rails for formwork
- Concrete
- F62 steel mesh and ties
- Mesh chairs
- Terracotta tiles 280 mm square
- Tile adhesive
- Tile grout
- Acid for etching

PREPARATION

1 Mark out the area, allowing for sufficient fall. Consider whether the dimensions accommodate full tiles.

2 Set finished height stringlines.

3 Excavate to a depth of 120 mm.

4 Use 100 x 50 mm timber to form up the area. Nail the formwork to pegs positioned outside the rails.

5 Prepare the concrete slab, making sure it is level and flat.

6 Finish the surface with a wooden float to create a slightly rough texture. Neaten with an edging tool.

7 Keep the slab moist for from five to seven days. Hose it down gently with water, then cover it completely with plastic. Allow adequate time for thorough curing.

CHOOSING AN ADHESIVE

8 Choose a flexible adhesive for strength or mix a mortar of three parts sand to one-part cement for ease of spreading or to disguise undulations in the concrete base.

Contrasting border inlays break up large expanses of terracotta tiles and can be used to reflect the colour scheme of nearby paintwork or plantings. Patient planning is necessary when calculating a detailed design.

A simple chequerboard pattern in sea green and white offsets the rich rusty tone of this terracotta-tiled porch.

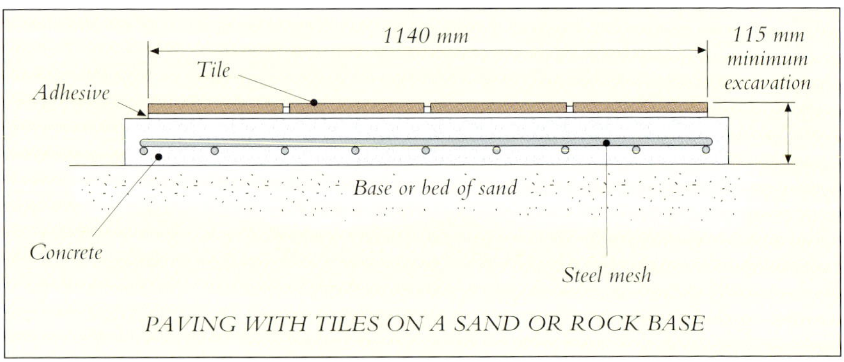

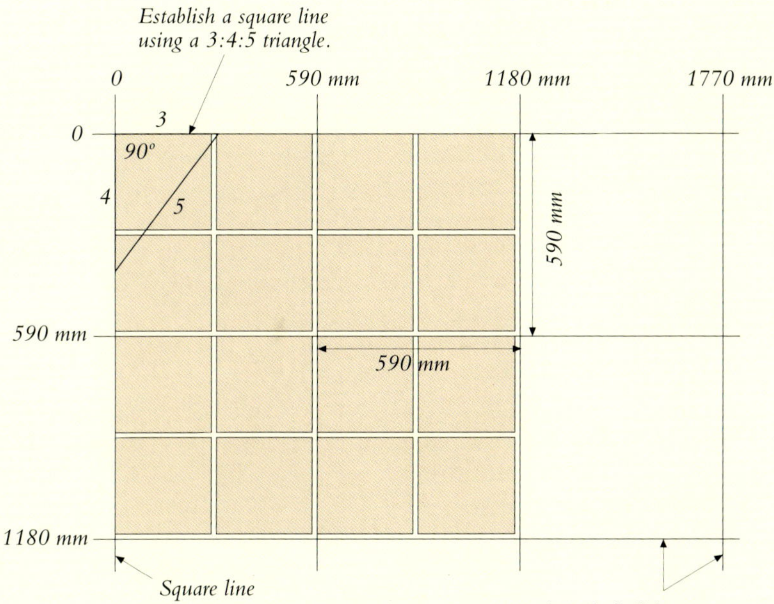

Grid = two tiles and two joints each way.

Based on four 280 mm square terracotta tiles per grid square.

Joint allowance 15 mm maximum.

SQUARE SET OUT

Lay the adhesive to a uniform depth. If the slab is level, create fall by graduating the adhesive or mortar from 30–40 mm to 10–20 mm.

SETTING OUT

9 Lay out the tiles to check that your selected pattern is possible with minimal cutting. Thin slivers of tile are difficult to cut so adjust the joints to correct the set-up.

Choose from two design options.

• For a square set out (see Square set out, above), measure the spacing of two standard paving tiles and their corresponding joints to determine the grid, then transfer this onto the base. Stretch a chalkline between the grid points and flick it to mark the

> HINT
>
> Terracotta tiles are surprisingly porous, so soak them in water for between twenty and thirty minutes (as recommended by the manufacturer) before laying. Dry tiles act like sponges, sucking moisture from the adhesive and weakening the paving bond.

concrete surface. Draw a 3:4:5 triangle in one corner to create a 90 degree angle. Measure the grid spacing in the opposite direction on both sides and continue marking. The time spent setting out a grid simplifies the laying process and saves unnecessary cutting, so work carefully to ensure your preferred pattern is achievable.

• To create a diagonal set out (see Diagonal set out, page 43), begin by laying a header course of, for example, rectangular half-tiles. Use a builder's square or measure a 3:4:5 triangle to ascertain that the first corner is square, so that the cuts required down the sides will not vary. Using a platform tile cutter, angle grinder or diamond-blade saw, cut several tiles into diagonal quarters and halves. Use a quarter-tile in one corner as the basis of your pattern. Establish that the area is square and mark a diagonal line from the back of the first corner tile. Draw this line as a 3:4:5 triangle and mark it in chalk. Mark a diagonal line perpendicular to the first, again based on a 3:4:5 triangle. Referring to these lines, continue ruling a 590 mm square grid. Lay out two rows then measure the spacing of two tiles and two joints each way to use as grid sizing.

HINT

Freshly laid concrete must be allowed to cure for several months before tiles or slate pavers are laid. The longer the curing time provided, the harder the finished base will be, with fewer cracks. As a rough guide, allowing at least one month for each 25 mm thickness of concrete is recommended.

CREATING A FIRM HOLD

10 Etch the slab with a mix of hydrochloric acid and water in a 1:10 ratio. (Always add the acid to the water—do not work in reverse). Spread the mix over the concrete and rub it firmly with a stiff-bristled broom. Rinse the slab with clean water and allow it to dry.

11 Work away from walls or other structures. To lay on the diagonal, start in one corner. Lay complete rows or cover one quarter at a time.

12 Mix sufficient tile adhesive for about 1 m^2 of tiles.

13 Using a metal float or bricklayer's trowel, spread adhesive onto the slab.

14 Use a 10–12 mm notched trowel held vertically to ridge the adhesive. Spread adhesive up to the grid lines.

LAYING THE TILES

15 Press each tile firmly onto the adhesive, twisting it slightly.

16 Tap the laid tiles gently with a rubber mallet to remove air bubbles. Continue tiling, leaving 10–12 mm gaps. Position the part-tiles as they occur or cut them in bulk later.

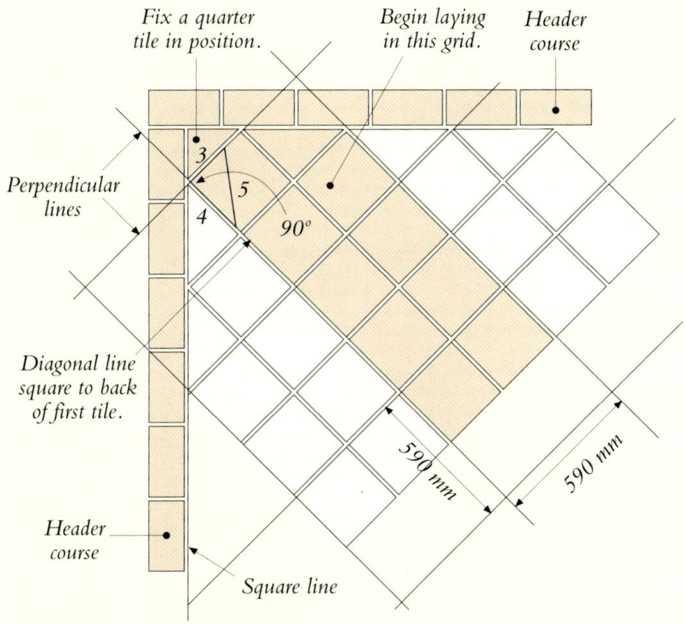

Grid = two tiles and two joints each way.
Based on four 280 mm square terracotta tiles per grid square.
Joint allowance 15 mm maximum.

DIAGONAL SET OUT

17 Keep the surface of the tiles free of adhesive by cleaning them with a damp sponge as you work.

18 Use a straight edge or spirit level to ensure the surface is even.

19 With a spirit level or straight edge, check the horizontal lines, making minor adjustments to the surface if necessary.

20 Allow the adhesive to set, then grout the joints. Purchase premixed grout from a tile retailer or mix your own by using fine-grained sand and cement with water in a 4:1 ratio. Work on an area of approximately 1 m^2 at a time.

21 Using a rubber squeegee or heavy sponge, work the mixture into the joints. Remove extra grout from the tile face with a moistened sponge. Allow the grout to set.

22 Once the grout has dried, give the tiled surface a final clean down, again using a large, clean sponge dipped in fresh water.

The addition of a white wrought iron setting and small terracotta pots transforms this verandah from casual to classy in just a few minutes, making slate the ideal material for multi-purpose spaces.

Slate paving

Slate paving works well in the creation of indoor–outdoor areas around the home. Courtyards, patios, entries, terraces and paths are all appropriate areas for the laying of slate.

TOOLS

- Basic tool kit (see page 17)
- 12 mm notched trowel
- Rubber hammer
- Large sponge or heavy-duty scouring pads
- Diamond-bladed brick saw or tungsten-bladed hack saw
- Broad-blade knife
- Bricklayer's trowel
- Buckets

PREPARATION

1 Mark out the area, allowing for sufficient fall.

2 The best base is concrete to a thickness of 100 mm with a light reinforcing mesh of F52 grade. Prepare the area and pour the concrete slab (see Laying a slab, page 34).

3 Concrete with a steel float finish must be acid-etched with a solution of one part hydrochloric acid to ten parts water and scarified lightly with a scutch hammer to improve bonding before paving is laid. If your slab has a wooden float finish, on the other hand, simply clean the surface (using an acid-etch, if necessary). Wear protective clothing. Once the fizzing subsides, use a stiff-bristled brush to loosen any surface grime. Rinse the area with fresh water.

4 Apply a suitable bonding agent.

MATERIALS

- Slate
- Adhesive
- Grout
- 100 x 50 mm rails for formwork
- Steel mesh and ties
- Mesh chairs
- Concrete
- Acid for etching
- Bonding agent
- Expansion joints

SETTING OUT

5 Separate the slate into three or four thickness groups. Place the thicker slate on the high side to drain surface water away from any buildings.

6 Lay out the slate, adjusting the joints to minimise cutting.

7 Establish a grid (see Establishing a grid, page 47). Ensure each square

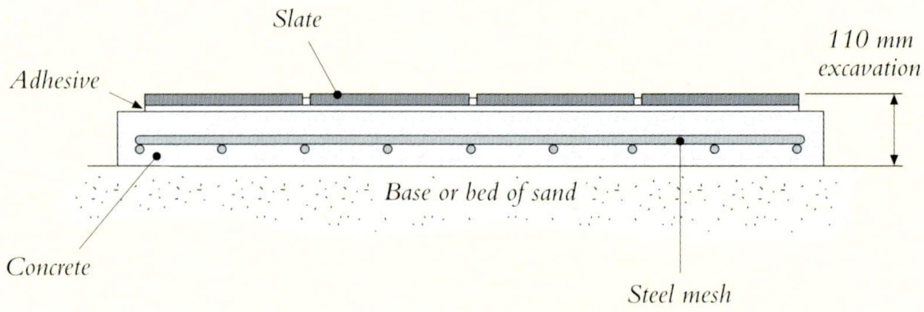

PAVING WITH SLATE ON A SAND OR ROCK BASE

contains two standard slate pavers and two joints in each direction.

8 Provide an expansion joint every 3600 mm in slate laid outdoors. Do not attempt to fit these joints exactly on the 3600 mm line—place them as appropriate within your chosen pattern.

CUTTING SLATE

9 When cutting slate, hire a diamond-bladed brick or wet saw, or use an angle grinder with a diamond blade or a tungsten blade fitted to a hack saw. Score the slate but do not attempt to snap it as laminations can cause it to break unpredictably.

LAYING THE SLATE

10 Mix the adhesive in a bucket, stirring until it is thick and creamy. For convenience, use a power drill with a blending attachment.

> HINT
>
> Do not lay slate in heavy outdoor traffic area such as driveways.

Leave the mix to stand for ten minutes (away from direct sunlight), then add extra powder or water if needed and remix. Mix sufficient adhesive to cover about one square metre at a time.

11 Spread the adhesive one block at a time. Work up to the grid lines but do not cover them.

12 Use a 12 mm notched trowel to spread the adhesive. Notch in one direction across the slab.

13 With a trowel, butter the base of each piece to form a solid bed.

14 Place the slate into position, pressing down with your palm and rocking gently back and forth to force trapped air out from beneath each paver. Air pockets produce a 'drummy' sound when the slate is tapped and can cause it to break away. Do not lay slate wet or onto a wet base, except when using a primer.
Lay chipped-edge slate face-down for a neater finish and easier grouting.

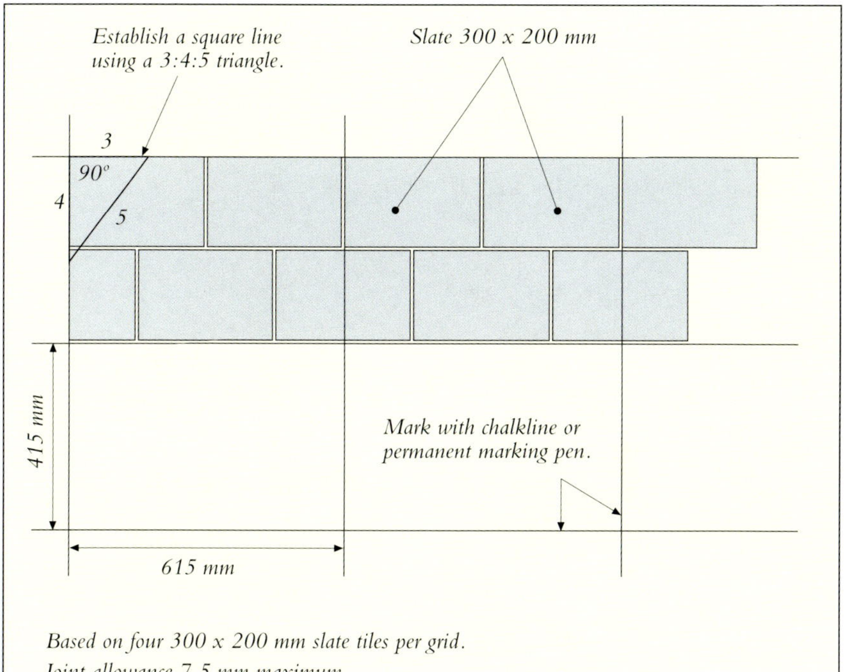

ESTABLISHING A GRID

15 Leave a 5–10 mm joint between slates but stay within the grid lines.

16 Clean the surface of the slate with water and a sponge as you work.

17 Allow the area to dry for between twenty-four and thirty-six hours before grouting.

GROUTING

18 Mix grout with sufficient water to form a firm paste.

19 Wet the surface of the slate. Work the grout into the joints by hand or with a squeegee.

20 Approximately every metre, clean away the excess grout. Squeeze clean water onto the paving, then drag a sponge diagonally across the joints. Rinse the sponge and repeat until the surface is clean.

21 Allow the grout to dry for at least twelve hours before walking on the fresh paving.

SEALING

22 Slate can be sealed after as few as seven days. In exterior areas, it is best left unsealed to avoid trapping efflorescence and other stains. Sealed slate turns slippery when wet.

Sandstone paving

Sandstone can be laid on a variety of bases: a dry mix of six parts sand to one part cement; a 50 mm bed of dry, washed river sand; or a concrete slab, using wet mortar.

TOOLS
• Basic tool kit (see page 17)
• Straight edge
• Dust mask and goggles for dry cutting

MATERIALS
• Split sandstone
• Coarse-grained bedding sand
• Concrete mix for edging
• Cement for grout
• Fine-grained sand for grout
• Mortar

PREPARATION

1 Make initial preparations and lay out the area. In this example, a random pattern known as 'crazy paving' is used.

2 Excavate the site, remembering that extra depth may be required to allow for variations in the stone.

3 Compact the soil. If the ground is spongy or of highly reactive clay, excavate for a further 100 mm and lay a bed of crushed rock.

4 Spread and screed a 50 mm layer of coarse-grained bedding sand.

5 Set up stringlines (or use pieces of rope as a guide for a curve).

6 Group the sandstone into piles of varying thickness.

LAYING THE STONE

7 Lay a straight-edged section of sandstone against the guiding edge to neaten what is otherwise an informal jigsaw pattern.If possible, lay the outer edges first, positioning the largest stones around the sides to create maximum strength in the design. Smaller stones tend to move under pressure and are best laid towards the centre.

8 Use your sense of perspective to fit the puzzle together. Leave a gap of

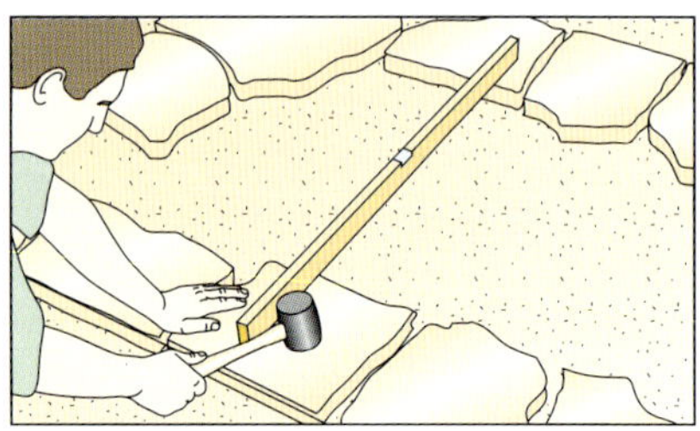

8 Tamp the pieces in place with a rubber mallet or softwood straight edge and lump hammer.

Sandstone is available in a choice of colours and patterns, ranging from subtle muted tones to this striking striated variation. It is most commonly laid in a random arrangement known as crazy paving or as neatly sawn square blocks.

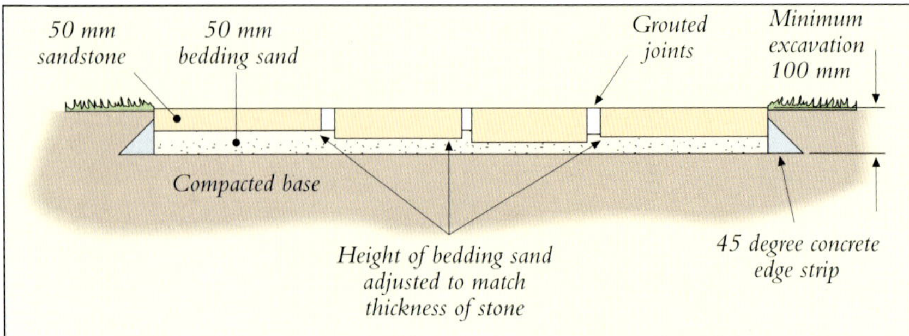

PAVING WITH SANDSTONE ON A COMPACTED BASE

about 10–20 mm for grouting. Adjust the depth of the bedding to accommodate stones of various thicknesses. Tamp the pieces in place with a rubber mallet or softwood straight edge and lump hammer, taking care to avoid chipping. Mortar the pieces into position.

9 Fill any remaining gaps with smaller pieces of sandstone mortared into place. If trimming is required, use a hammer and bolster to maintain the split appearance; do not be tempted to cut the stone.

10 Check the finished level, then tamp the stone once more by hand.

11 Edge the area (see Providing an edge, pages 13–15).

12 Grout the freshly laid sandstone using one of two methods.

- Spread a dry mix of 6:1 fine-grained sand and cement and sweep it into the joints. Remove the excess and hose lightly with a fine spray.
- Mix a very stiff mortar and push it neatly into the joints, using a trowel. Smooth with a small paintbrush moistened with fresh water. Clean the face of the sandstone with a large, lightly dampened sponge. Change the water regularly to prevent staining the stone.

HINT

Sandstone is heavy! For example, an 800 x 400 x 50 mm paving slab weighs approximately 38 kg. Sandstone is easiest to move and lay when two people work together but remember to take care when handling the corners as they break off easily.

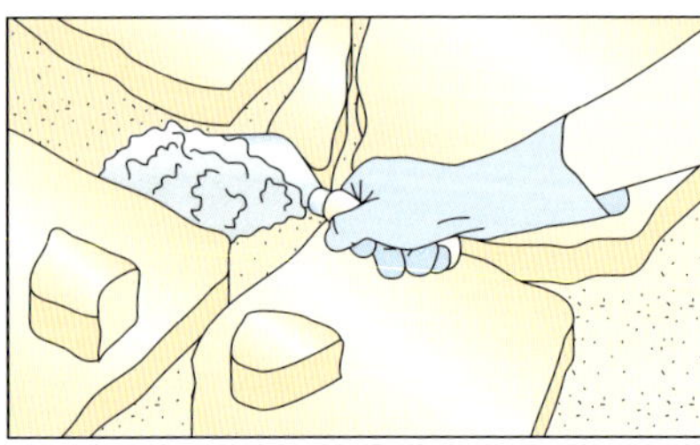

9 Fill any remaining gaps with smaller pieces of sandstone mortared into position.

SANDSTONE PAVING ON CONCRETE

No material surpasses solid concrete as a base for paving. Under sandstone pavers, the stability of a concrete slab prevents movement and cracking.

PREPARATION

1 Mark out the area, allowing for sufficient fall.

2 Set finished-height stringlines.

3 Excavate the site to a depth of approximately 180 mm.

4 Set up the formwork, place F62 steel mesh inside the area and pour the concrete.

5 Cut sandstone with a brick saw or hammer and bolster. If it is too thick to be split in the conventional manner, cut mid-way through each piece with a circular saw and masonry blade, then force the stone open with wedges or a bolster. As an alternative, lay the sandstone over a piece of metal angle-iron and tap the back until it splits.

Freshly sawn stone has sharp edges which must be rubbed with another piece of sandstone to prevent chipping.

MIXING MORTAR

6 Mix a mortar of 4:1 fine-grained sand and cement. Add an agent (such as Bycol) to make the mix light and workable.

7 Spread the mixture to form a 20–30 mm bed.

8 Dust the mortar with dry cement and wet the back of each sandstone piece with water or a bonding agent mixed with water.

LAYING THE STONE

9 Work outwards from a solid structure or corner, following perpendicular stringlines.

10 Align each stone carefully. Butt the pieces together, leaving a gap of 1–2 mm for expansion. Do not allow the edges or corners to touch as they chip easily. Lay the stones one row at a time. Move the stringlines regularly to check the alignment.

11 Adjust the stones by tamping with a softwood straight edge and mallet to form an even surface. Check using a spirit level.

12 Edge the area with a material of your choice (see Providing an edge, pages 13–15).

13 Spread the area with fine-grained sand or a dry mix of 6:1 sand and cement and sweep it into the joints.

Dry-bedding concrete pavers

Large pavers cover a surface area quickly and can be laid in a choice of ways. Pavers laid on a compacted base of crushed rock or concrete are easily bedded on coarse-grained sand.

MATERIALS

- 100 x 50 mm rails for formwork
- F62 steel mesh and ties
- Mesh chairs
- Concrete
- Concrete pavers (400 x 400 mm x 40 mm)

TOOLS

- Basic tool kit (see page 17)
- Bolt cutters or angle grinder
- Brick saw
- Pliers or wire twitcher
- Buckets
- Wooden float
- Cement mixer
- Squeegee
- Rubber gloves

PREPARATION

1 Mark out and prepare the area (see Preparation, page 27).

2 The square format of large pavers limits possible patterns to stretcher or stack bond, with an optional inlay.

3 Set up stringlines and a grid to guide your paving, and establish a definite laying face (see Setting out, pages 41–2). When paving around a solid structure or square corner, always work outwards to avoid having to cut pavers to fill awkward spaces.

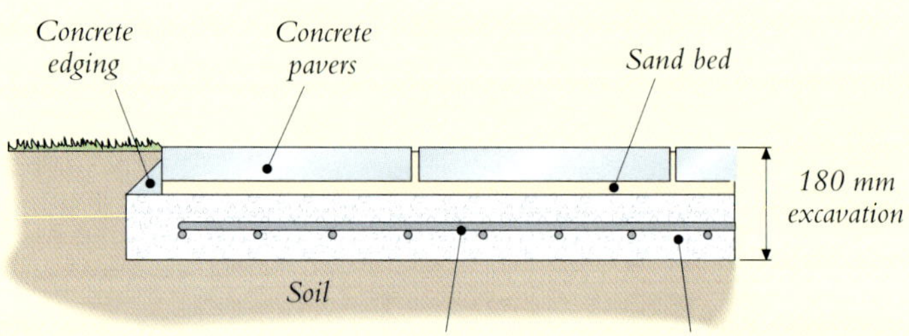

DRY-BEDDING ON A CONCRETE BASE

Fine-grained sand is the only grout required in this waterside location, laid with imitation limestone pavers. The faux stone finish is just one of many developed by the manufacturers of modern concrete products.

4 Leave a 5–10 mm grouting joint. Use spacers cut from fibro cement or cardboard to keep the joints even.

5 Check the level and tamp if needed.

LAYING THE PAVERS

6 Lay the full pavers first, then fill the remaining gaps with cut sections. For convenience, use a diamond-bladed brick saw when cutting heavy concrete pavers.

7 Grout with fine-grained, dry sand.

8 Compact with a plate compactor, taking care not to damage the pavers.

9 Lay your choice of edging (see Providing an edge, pages 13–15).

Wet-bedding concrete pavers

Pavers laid on a solid concrete slab can be set on compacted sand or, preferably, wet-bedded for stability onto a base of freshly mixed mortar.

MATERIALS

- 100 x 50 mm rails for formwork
- F62 steel mesh
- Ties and mesh chairs
- Concrete
- Sand and cement for mortar and slurry
- Concrete pavers (400 x 400 mm x 40 mm)
- Elasticiser

TOOLS

- Basic tool kit (see page 17)
- Bolt cutters or angle grinder
- Brick saw
- Pliers or wire twitcher
- Buckets
- Wooden float
- Cement mixer
- Squeegee
- Rubber gloves

PREPARATION

1 Mark out the area.

2 Excavate to a depth of 180 mm below the finished stringline height.

3 Set up formwork and pour the concrete. Allow the slab to dry.

4 Sweep the base and acid etch.

5 Set up stringlines and grids to control the laying sequence.

MIXING MORTAR

6 Mix a 3:1 mortar of three parts fine-grained washed sand to one part cement, with an elasticiser added.

7 Dampen the concrete and spread a slurry of six-parts cement to one-part sand, or sprinkle neat cement over the concrete and spray gently with water. Sweep the surface lightly.

8 Set up screed rails and level the wet mortar mix to a depth of 25–30 mm.

9 Sprinkle neat cement over the wet mortar, then moisten and trowel it.

LAYING THE PAVERS

10 Coat the back of each paver with slurry. Bed and tamp it into position to the finished stringline height.

11 Leave a 5–10 mm joint between the pavers for grouting.

12 Place a straight edge over the surface to check for level.

Small concrete pavers set on a bed of wet mortar are easily manoeuvred into position to create several levels on sloping ground. In this courtyard, they provide a clean, dry surface in a naturally damp and shady spot.

13 Lay full pavers, then fill any remaining gaps with cut sections.

14 Allow the paving to dry for at least twelve hours, keeping it covered and moist to prevent cracking.

15 Prepare a grout mix, adding a colourant if desired, and mix it to a workable consistency.

16 Moisten the joints with a wet sponge and use a rubber squeegee to push the grout into place until it is flush with the tops of the pavers.

17 Remove excess grout and clean the pavers with a damp sponge.

18 Edge the paving with the method of your choice.

Paving around pools

Bullnose coping pavers form a smooth, child-safe edging around swimming pools and formal ponds. Plan curved layouts carefully to ensure your chosen pattern fits neatly into the space provided.

TOOLS

- Basic tool kit (see page 17)
- Tools appropriate to your chosen material and method of laying

MATERIALS

- Pavers and associated materials
- Two-pack epoxy resin or solvent-based adhesive (for fibreglass pool) or sand, cement and bonding agent (for concrete pool)
- Coping material

CHOOSING MATERIALS

Square or rectangular pools have a formal appearance and look great set in cut stone, tiles, or clay or concrete pavers laid in regular geometric patterns. Free-flowing, natural-looking pools work well in a less formal setting of crazy paving, split stone, flagging or rumbled pavers.

Coping pavers are usually available in three basic shapes: half-bullnose, bullnose and coper.

POOL EDGES

The edging of a swimming pool can be either submerged or raised.

- Submerged edges lie below the waterline, creating a 'swim out' effect. As the selected paving material is constantly wet, special water-resistant adhesives are required. Consult your supplier for advice on fixing pavers under these conditions.
- Raised coping sits above the waterline in a step-like effect around the edge of the pool. Most pools are constructed in this way with the paving fixed horizontally to a fibreglass or concrete surface. Choose an adhesive manufactured to withstand the constant lapping of water against the edge.

PREPARATION

1 Plan your paving to accentuate the pool's outline. Remember that achieving a neat finish is important. Pay particular attention to proposed cuts on corners and sharp curves.

2 Pre-cut your paving and lay out the coping. This is time-consuming but potential problems can be corrected with relative ease at this early stage.

3 When laying raised coping over fibreglass, select an adhesive to suit both your paving material and the situation. These range from two-pack epoxy resins (such as Flexifix)

Select a coping material and surround that blend harmoniously into the broader garden landscape. The warm-toned clay pavers in this setting complement the poolside collection of terracotta planters.

and solvent-based adhesives (such as Liquid Nails) for fibreglass to a 3:1 mix of sand and cement combined with a bonding agent for concrete. Consult your local supplier.

4 Improve keying by running a grinder lightly over the fibreglass to roughen the surface.

5 Identify a starting point. This can be anywhere around the side of an oval or round pool, but remember to manipulate the joint gaps in the last 2 m to eliminate unnecessary cutting. Rectangular or square pools are best worked from corner to corner. Pre-cut and lay the corners, then space the pavers evenly in between. Adjust the gaps to accommodate uncut, full pavers where possible. Treat irregularly shaped pools similarly, laying the corners first and modifying the joints to suit the pavers. If it is not possible to complete the design with full pavers alone, trim narrow widths from three or four pavers instead of removing a larger—and more noticeable—slice from just one.

LAYING

6 Mix the adhesive according to the manufacturer's instructions and apply it to the top edge of the pool.

7 Press each paver into the adhesive, making sure the surface fall is away from the edging to prevent loose debris entering the water. Allow the pavers to overlap the edge by 15–20 mm to minimise splash onto the surrounding surface.

8 From time to time, check the level.

9 Grout the joints either a section at a time or at the end.

10 Clean the surface of the pavers as you work, using a wet sponge and clean water. Remove all traces of adhesive and any mortar stains and allow the paving to dry for twenty-four hours.

11 When you are sure the area is dry, paint the mortared joints with a bonding agent to seal them and prevent deterioration. Repeat this at regular intervals as part of your pool maintenance routine.

12 Once the coping is in place it provides an edge for the remainder of the pool surround. Prepare and pave this as you would any other open area, following the line of the coping with a suitable stretcher bond.

> HINT
>
> Salt attack occurs when water splashed from a salt-chlorinated pool onto pavers. As the water evaporates, salt crystals form. When these dry and are added to by more splashing, they enlarge, damaging the surface of many paving materials. Some products offer increased resistance to salt, so seek your supplier's advice.

PAVING AROUND PONDS

The surround or edge of any pond can reflect either a formal or an informal design.

PREPARATION

Formal designs are built on regular geometric shapes, found in sandstone slabs, house bricks, clay pavers, slate pieces and tiles. Informal designs are accentuated by the rustic appearance of railway sleepers and the natural look of rock, cobbles and plants.

A pond used to attract wading birds or animal life requires a vastly different approach to that of one designed to withstand the pressure of humans walking or sitting on the edge.

In formal settings, the water level usually rests just below the edging. Ensure the capping material is parallel to the surface.

Use materials that blend with the landscape or create contrast by choosing colours or textures that differ from those nearby.

It is difficult to mortar bricks, cut stone, tiles or slate directly to the plastic liners used in many ponds, so construct walls or footings of brick or concrete before laying the capping. Use a concrete footing which doubles as a floor to add stability beneath brick or concrete walls. Paint the inner surface with a waterproofing agent to seal the pond.

When mortaring a capping onto a pond wall, use a bonding agent in the mix to improve adhesion and waterproofing.

CHOOSING AN EDGING

As water often overlaps informal edges, the edging material is usually submerged. Use a plastic liner to create a natural-looking free-form pond. Position the perimeter of the liner above the anticipated water-level before laying your chosen edging material around the side. Batter a buttress of concrete to hold it in place. Informal rock edges look natural as flowing curves. A partly submerged boulder adds interest at the water's edge.

Cut timber to any shape to create a useful edge where a pond surround is extended into a deck. Use timber vertically along the edges by setting treated logs on end in the ground.

Allow water to lap at natural-looking gravel or pebbles planted to harmonise with the landscape. Use rock or timber paving to strengthen soft edges to withstand foot traffic.

ADDING FEATURES

Install a small fountain, a statue, a running tap from a reticulating pump or a small bridge to give your project a professional finish.

A series of broad sandstone steps eases the transition from lawn to paved driveway on this sloping block. The uneven number and the depth of these steps make them both attractive and practical as a garden feature.

Paving steps

Whether designed to cope with a sloping site or to terrace a yard, steps or ramps add relief to the landscape. Choosing materials in keeping with the environment makes them less obtrusive.

TOOLS

- Basic tool kit (see page 17)
- Cement mixer (if mixing your own)
- Square-nosed shovel
- Gumboots
- Edger
- Wooden float

MATERIALS

- Clay pavers (or house bricks)
- Timber formwork
- Timber pegs
- Nails
- Concrete
- Bonding agent

DESIGNING STEPS

When designing steps that will be functional and attractive, combine a 150 mm riser with a 350 mm tread. Provide a 5–10 mm fall to the front to prevent water pooling. (Modify these dimensions if desired.)

Gradual steps laid on gentle inclines can be fitted with treads deeper than the standard 350 mm, enabling walkers to step twice or more on each level. Steep steps are necessary on sharply inclining ground. Build these with one-step treads and install a handrail for safety.

Stepped ramps are appropriate on long, gentle inclines. Place risers vertically to break up the surface.

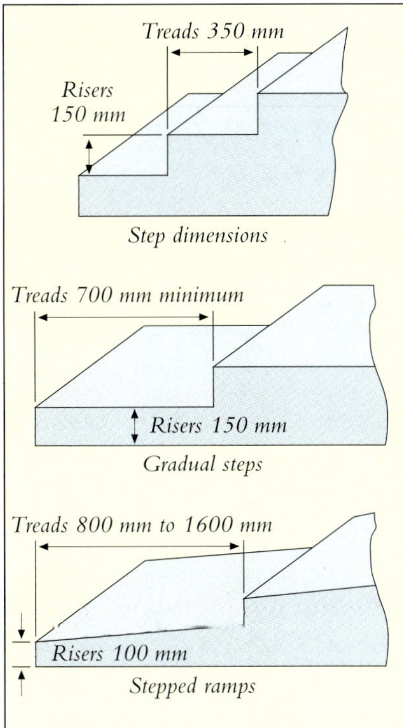

TYPES OF STEPS

BUILDING A SINGLE STEP

1 Using 100 x 50 mm timber, form up the front and side edges of the step. Peg the timber formwork firmly into position.

2 Mix and pour the concrete to the top of the formwork. Level the surface with a wooden float, leaving a rough finish.

3 Allow the concrete to dry for two or three days, then remove the formwork boards.

4 To create a riser, butter the reverse face of a paver with mortar and tap it firmly into position against the vertical concrete face. Improve adhesion by painting the paver and concrete with a bonding agent and water mixed in equal parts.

5 Mortar the treads into position, creating a 5–10 mm fall to the front. Ensure the treads overhang their risers by 15–20 mm. Lay a second row of pavers, running in the opposite direction.

RAMPS

Ramps are an alternative to several steps when negotiating inclines or changes in level on sloping ground.

For the sake of safety and convenience, the length of a wheelchair ramp must vary depending on the rate of incline.

RATE OF INCLINE	RAMP LENGTH
1:33	25 m
1:20	14 m
1:14	9 m
1:8	1.25 m

The average ramp should be sloped at 1:14, to a length of 9 m. Refer to the Standards Australia guidelines for further information.

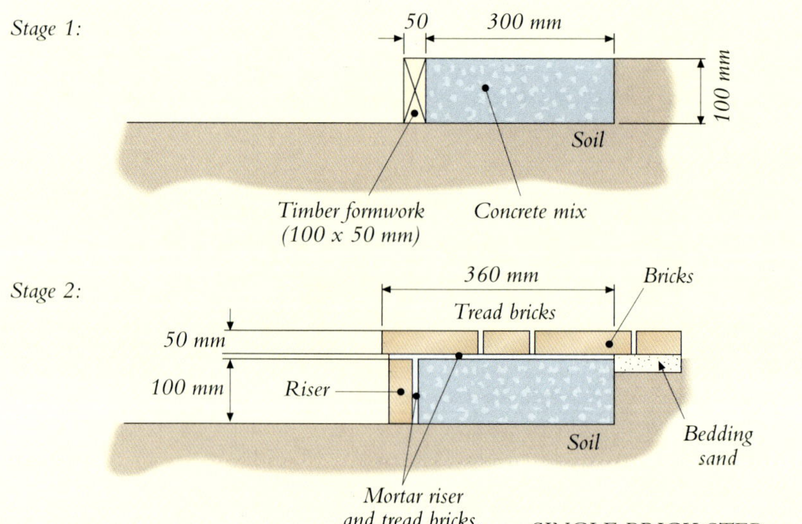

SINGLE BRICK STEP

Tools for paving

Some of the most useful tools for laying pavers are shown below. Build up your tool kit gradually—most of the tools can be purchased from your local hardware or paving store.

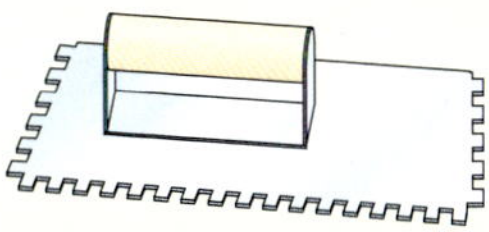

NOTCHED TROWEL
Used for spreading and ribbing a bed of adhesive

SCUTCH HAMMER
Hammer with comb-like teeth on one end for chipping bricks

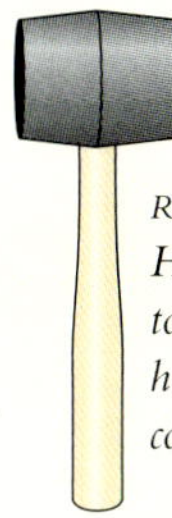

RUBBER MALLET
Hammer-like tool with rubber head for compacting pavers

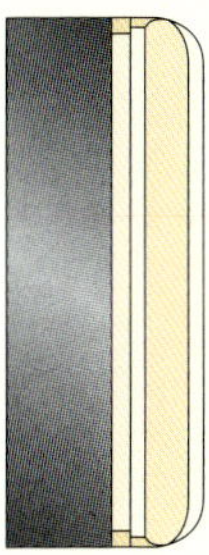

RUBBER SQUEEGEE
Rubber-bladed tool used for spreading grout over tiles

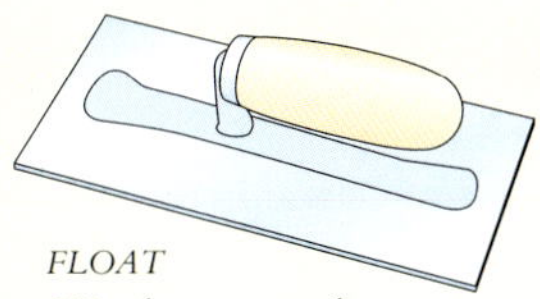

FLOAT
Wooden or metal tool for smoothing and compressing wet concrete

BOLSTER
Cold chisel with a broad splade for cutting pavers, bricks or stone

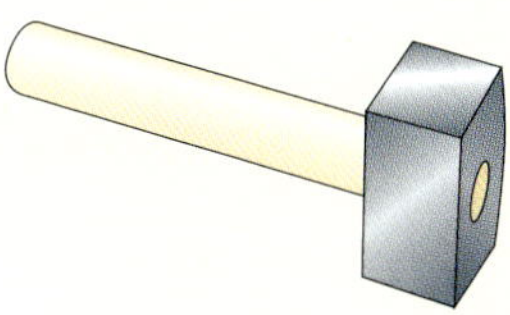

LUMP HAMMER
Small, heavy type of mallet used with a straight edge for compacting pavers

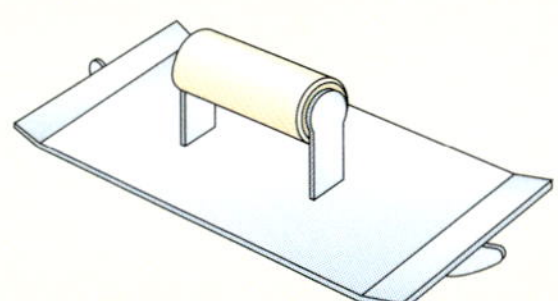

JOINTING TOOL
Used for creating control joints in fresh concrete to allow for expansion

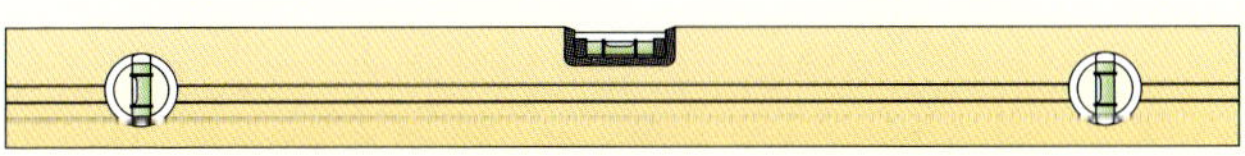

SPIRIT LEVEL *Block containing a sealed tube in which an air bubble rests between two marks when placed horizontally*

Index